PIECES *of* FAITH

Rebecca Nolting

PIECES

of

FAITH

*Discovering God in
My Life Puzzle*

ASK PUBLISHING
Pueblo, Colorado

Pieces of Faith: Discovering God in My Life Puzzle

ASK Publishing books may be purchased in bulk at special discounts for sales promotion, corporate gifts, ministry, fundraising, or educational purposes. Special editions can also be created to specifications. For details, contact rebecca@extraordinaryfromordinary.com.

Visit our website at www.extraordinaryfromordinary.com.

ISBN: 978-1-7376370-0-4
E-book: 978-1-7376370-1-1

Cover and interior design by Marisa Jackson for TLC Book Design, TLCBookDesign.com.

TABLE OF CONTENTS

ACKNOWLEDGMENTS

First, I want to thank God for always being with me, especially when I didn't recognize him. There were many moments that I felt his presence while writing this, and this is my way to praise him.

Second, I want to thank Pastor Scott Schurle for being willing to read my drafts, especially the first two! Your encouragement and feedback helped push me to "finish the task."

Third, a huge thank you to the team at TLC Book Design. Tamara has been patient with me. I have sent her many emails, and I felt her prayers as I pushed through the challenges. Her editor, Misti Moyer, helped fix all my writing habits I never knew I had and made me sound much smarter than I am. She challenged me to make it even better, and I am grateful for that. Her designer, Marisa Jackson, took my vision and turned it into something wonderful. She went above and beyond what I even imagined it would be.

Next, I want to thank Roseanne Cheng, who gave me great advice and connected me with the team at TLC Book Design. Her support meant a lot, even if I didn't write a book about teenage vampires. (I had to sneak that in somehow!)

Thanks also to the countless people who helped guide me on my faith journey, including family, friends, and church leaders who have shown me the love of Jesus.

Finally, I want to thank my husband Jeffrey for his support throughout the whole process. This is a new adventure for me, and I could not have done it without him.

LETTER FROM REBECCA

Dear Friend,

I'm guessing if you've picked up this book, you might be at a crossroads in your faith journey. Maybe you're just starting out, or you've been practicing for a long time. I understand that feeling of being overwhelmed, confused, and even doubtful. If that's you, you're in the right place. I am by no means an expert on the topic of faith, and I don't pretend to have all the answers. I still have a lot to learn.

I have always enjoyed expressing myself through writing, with poetry and journaling as a teenager and short stories more recently. In 2016, I started the blog *Extraordinary from Ordinary*. I chose this name because God is in everything, even the most common things, if we look for him. God makes those things extraordinary. I am just a regular person who has had the normal ups and downs of life. But as Priscilla Shirer said, "He puts extraordinary tasks on the plates of ordinary people so that ordinary people can see what an extraordinary God can do through them...The enemy's voice says, 'You don't have enough. You're not able. You can't.' The voice of the Holy Spirit says, 'I have enough. I am able through you. I can!'"[1] I can admit that there is no way that I have written this on my own. God has been with me the entire time as my guide.

---

1 Priscilla Shirer, *Discerning the Voice of God: How to Recognize When God Is Speaking*, rev. ed. (Nashville, Tennessee: LifeWay Press, 2017), p. 157.

While working on a puzzle, I couldn't help but notice the similarities between the challenges of putting together a puzzle and one's faith journey. This includes the ups and downs, the obstacles and the successes. All these moments can and will shape someone's faith journey. Since "we live by faith, not by sight" (2 Cor. 5:7, New International Version), I hope that some of the ordinary objects and stories in my life can help someone else deepen his or her faith or explore it in a new way. Or, as the Casting Crowns sing:

"Just to know You and to make You known…
We know we were made for so much more than ordinary lives
It's time for us to more than just survive
We were made to thrive"[2]

This book is called *Pieces of Faith* because my faith has helped me overcome the challenges and hurdles I have faced. These events have strengthened my faith and given me peace. These stories will hopefully help you piece together what God's will is for your own life.

I have included questions at the end of each chapter for you to think and reflect on. You can use them as part of your meditation, prayer, and/or journaling. Writing about my own faith story has strengthened my relationship with God, and I want the same for you. You don't have to be a professional writer to tell your story. You just have to be open and willing to let the Spirit move you. Let's get moving!

Rebecca

---

2 Casting Crowns, "Thrive," Track 1 on *Thrive*, Provident Label Group, 2013, compact disc.

ONE

TAKE THE FIRST STEP

"If you can trust a puzzle company to make sure
every piece is in the box to complete the puzzle,
then why can't you trust GOD that every piece of
your life is there for a reason?"[3]

The first step of faith is the hardest. The day we got a puzzle in the mail for my husband Jeffrey's birthday was the same day I quit my job as a home health scheduler. I had been there for seven years, starting first as a caregiver and then moving up to working in the office. When I started that job, I was so grateful to have supervisors who were appreciative and positive. The last year of working

---

3 @thedailyscripturedose, "Today in church, Pastor said this: If you can trust a puzzle company," Instagram, February 17, 2019, https://www.instagram.com/p/Bt_DzaAlK_9/.

there, many things had changed, including me. As I gained confidence in myself and found my voice, I felt more and more stifled at my job. I had conflicting feelings about the decision, but I knew, in my heart, it was right. The risk was worth taking because of the peace and freedom I received.

Like starting a new puzzle, I decided to take the first step, even though it interrupted my life. I wasn't planning on quitting without having another job lined up, but I felt like I heard a whisper that said, "It'll be ok." It is similar to when Abram (later named Abraham) was told, "Go from your country, your people and your father's household to the land I will show you" (Gen. 12:1). It wasn't a complete step-by-step guide to the rest of his life. Just the first step. Joyce Meyer addressed this when she said, "As was true of Abraham, God has given each of us a 'degree of faith.' For whatever we need to do, we have the faith to do it; but for faith to work, we have to release our faith, and the way we release it is to go in obedience. We have to go with our dreams despite all the 'what ifs' and the doubts from the enemy. When we make our step, God shows up."[4]

Now my story is not as drastic by any means, but it still has a first step of faith. While I chose to disrupt my life, I didn't know what would be in the future. I don't know how Abram felt the moment he chose to follow God's command: fear, anxiety, excitement, peace, perhaps a combination of them all. The important thing is that he listened and obeyed. Beth Moore said, "Coincidences are miracles where God chooses to remain anonymous."[5] Since there are no real coincidences, two weeks after quitting my job, our ladies'

---

4 Joyce Meyer, *The Confident Woman Devotional: 365 Daily Inspirations* (New York, New York: FaithWorks, 2010), p. 21.

5 Beth Moore, *Esther*, Introductory Video (LifeWay Press, Nashville, Tennessee, 2008).

Bible study started *Discerning the Voice of God* by Priscilla Shirer. From these lessons, I felt an urge to write. Even though I have felt this before, it's about God's timing and making the choice to listen to that voice and obey. The writing process started a new part of my journey. I reflected on many events in my life that influenced who I am today, from the more recent to those first steps in my faith journey.

My first steps in faith began when I was baptized as an infant and went through the other sacraments of the Catholic Church: First Communion, Confirmation, and Reconciliation (Penance). I also attended Catholic school from kindergarten through eighth grade. We went to Mass every week, and when I got to high school, I was very active in youth group. I was given the foundation of faith at a young age, which I am grateful for. But it is through the testing of faith that we see how strong our faith is.

My faith story truly begins on the day I was born. I have been told that my birth was considered traumatic because it happened so quickly. I started having seizures soon after, and my parents were scared because they couldn't figure out why it was happening. My parents received this advice: "One day, a friend reminded me that we shouldn't pray to God to make everything okay, but instead pray for strength to accept whatever the outcome and love you for as long as God allowed you to be entrusted to our care."[6] Thankfully, my parents trusted and listened to this friend. The seizures stopped once they put me on medication. After a few months, I was taken off the medication and was okay. So, my parents' faith is how my faith story began.

---

6 Personal letter from my parents, March 24, 2017.

I have had only had a handful of seizures since then, all before I turned nineteen and only when I have hit my head hard enough to trigger one. Each time, I was doing something ordinary—riding my bike, basketball practice, general playing, and driving. Then I would hit my head at some point (memories are foggy at best), and my life was interrupted for at least a few hours. I imagine it was scarier for those around me as they didn't know how to help me. Thankfully, in each of the instances, I was able to walk away with only minor injuries. This included a one-car accident at age eighteen when we were able to avoid getting hit or hitting anyone else. My guardian angel has been protecting me all my life.

Except for one time, when I hit my head and had a seizure, I was checked out by EMS and went to the emergency room. I also had to see a neurologist to make sure everything was okay, which usually included an order for an EEG. I have had both normal and abnormal results, but the one I was most thankful for was the last normal test. It was after that car accident, and they were more than likely going to recommend medication if the results were abnormal. Now, I do see the benefit of necessary medication, like when I was an infant. But in this case, I was happy the results were normal.

One reason I feel compelled to share this as part of my faith story is many years ago, I woke up in the middle of the night and felt I heard a whisper from God: epilepsy (seizures). I had no idea why this particular word, so I thought maybe it had to do with God's will for my life, but I didn't see how. Most people don't know this part of my life. It's kind of a weird icebreaker when meeting someone. Looking back, I can see it's one of the reasons my faith has grown. I am grateful for the many times I could have been hurt so much worse but was protected instead. My first steps in faith prepared me for all my future steps.

The second reason I wanted to share about my history of seizures is you don't always know what someone is going through. They may look fine on the outside, but they may struggle with mental health issues or past addictions. Many of these often come with a stigma that makes it difficult for people to talk about. Fortunately, God has forgiven all your sins through Jesus and loves you for who you are. You are not defined by any one condition or diagnosis. There is a story in Matthew about Jesus healing the sick, including those having seizures. I believe something happened after I was taken off the medication, some may call it a miracle, that stopped my seizures as an infant. This part of my life has made me more empathetic to others who are going through it.

I was asked recently if the seizures still haunt me. I had never considered that because it has always been part of my life. While I don't have to face it on a daily basis, that is not the same reality for others. We each have our own unique path. Faith requires us to let go of what could have been or even wishing we didn't have to deal with it ourselves. Taking the first step of embracing your story, with all the weaknesses or "faults" or diagnoses, is the beginning of letting the peace of God into your life.

It's hard to describe how it feels to have a seizure, even if you have had one. The medical definition of a seizure is a "sudden, uncontrolled electrical disturbance in the brain."[7] This unplanned interruption can feel like how you feel about your faith in some moments. You want to maintain control and organization over

7 "Seizures." Mayo Clinic. Accessed May 9, 2021. https://www.mayoclinic.org/diseases-conditions/seizure/symptoms-causes/syc-20365711.

your life, but God has something better in mind. Putting together a puzzle includes concrete pieces you can see and touch, and you develop a strategy to complete the picture. Unlike a puzzle, faith is one step of trust at a time because you cannot see all the pieces and how they fit together. Sometimes it can feel more like a giant leap. Even if your faith feels disorganized or chaotic, like having a seizure, you can find peace in God.

So, whether pursuing your calling, telling others your story of faith, or simply starting a new puzzle, you have to decide to take that first step, even if it feels like an unplanned interruption. As Maya Angelou said, "Not everything you create will be a masterpiece, but you get out there and try and sometimes it really happens. The other times you're just stretching your soul."[8] So here we go!

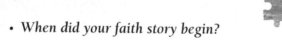

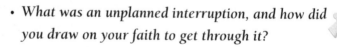

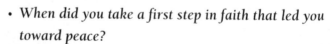

- *When did your faith story begin?*
- *What was an unplanned interruption, and how did you draw on your faith to get through it?*
- *When did you take a first step in faith that led you toward peace?*

---

8 Maya Angelou. Placard. August 2004.

TWO

FOLLOW THE SIGNS

"Trust in the Lord with all your heart and lean not
on your own understanding; in all your ways submit
to him, and he will make your paths straight."

(PROV. 3:5-6)

Once you decide to start a puzzle, the second step is deciding on the number of pieces and the picture. The puzzle we got was a Route 66 puzzle with cars and license plates of the states the highway goes through. The most iconic piece of Route 66 is the sign—you recognize it immediately. Wouldn't it be nice if all signs showing which path to take were that blatantly obvious? Instead, you have to discern what the signs in your life are showing you on your path, especially when it comes to faith.

You follow the first sign when you accept Jesus as your Savior. Once saved, there are many more signs on your faith journey.

This first sign is spoken of in the Bible: "Enter through the narrow gate. For wide is the gate and broad is the road that leads to destruction, and many enter through it. But small is the gate and narrow the road that leads to life, and only a few find it" (Matt. 7:13-14). This refers to the path people have chosen for themselves: to go with the way of the world (broad road) or to follow Jesus (narrow road). I believe to stay on the path, you must choose the right way.

I wish that I could say that I chose to stay active in church, which is part of the narrow path. When I moved away for college, I started attending the campus Catholic Church. It helped me transition to living on my own. Unfortunately, I saw a few members being judgmental and exclusionary. Their decision to exclude someone from participating in a retreat appeared intentionally hurtful. This didn't feel like the way Christians should act towards one another, so I stopped attending. Unfortunately, I think most people probably have similar examples of those who use unchristian-like words and actions. What seems to look like a bad sign can also show us what a good one is supposed to look like. I was also at a point in my life where I was trying to figure out who I was and what path to take in my career. Even though I wasn't actively involved in a church community for about five years, I still had my faith.

A few years later, I followed the signs I was given and moved to Colorado. I had graduated from Sacramento State with my bachelor's in social work and tried to secure a job in Fresno to be closer to my boyfriend of three-and-a-half years. Instead, he broke up with me. I was devastated. The plan that I thought I had for my life was completely interrupted. Like many of the people in the Bible, I didn't know then where my path would lead me. They probably thought they knew what their life plan was, but then God threw a curveball, like sending Jonah to Nineveh. Jonah had to spend time in a whale to agree to God's plan rather than sticking with his own. While I was trying to figure out what I was going to do next, I got a nudge (a sign) from my parents to apply to graduate school. Since I didn't have any reason to stay where I was, I was willing to take that turn. I chose the University of Denver because that was where my undergraduate internship supervisor had gone. I had never before considered moving to Colorado. I left everything and everyone I knew and moved to an apartment in Denver. It was scary to be alone.

There were many Sundays that I tried to get back on the narrow path. I had gotten out of the routine of being involved, and it was easy not to make it a priority. I attended a few different churches in Sacramento and Denver, but it was a struggle to find one without comparing it to the church I grew up in. None seemed to measure up to the standards I had in my head. After I met Jeffrey and made the move to Pueblo, Colorado, we began contemplating attending a church together. After attending a few different churches, we had been invited to play volleyball at a Disciples of Christ church. This denomination made both of us feel comfortable with our different backgrounds (mine was Catholic and his was Baptist). We were welcomed by a lady named Pat Flynn. It was the first church we both wanted to go to again, which was a sign this was a good fit for us. It was important for us to get on the same path together as we began our marriage. We then started including attending church on Sundays into our routine. We were on our way to building our relationship with God together.

We have since joined that church and slowly became involved in many areas. Pat took me under her wing. She wanted to train me to be the worship team leader. She saw the potential in me before I did and could see a path for me to use my God-given gifts. I resisted taking on this role for a few years, but I eventually agreed. I am so grateful for finding this church and Pat's guidance. She helped me increase my confidence in speaking my opinion and being a good leader in the church.

While traveling on this path of leadership, I have overcome obstacles and challenges. One of the biggest challenges was when we couldn't meet in person. We had to get creative about how to get a message out to our congregation and others. After a few weeks of live streaming music, Scripture, sermons, and Communion, our pastor suggested that we add an elder message. During our regular Sunday service, we had an elder of the church give a short devotion before we collected our offering. Since I was also walking out my faith as an elder, I was asked to do it. Here was the one that made a big change in my life:

Back in January 2020, our worship team discussed whether we should continue putting Pastor Scott's sermons on YouTube. We agreed that even though only a few people were watching it, we would continue. What we didn't know then was this would be the way we would "gather" as a congregation on Sundays for a while. But God knew. Our church had also just updated our directory with current contact information for all members. We didn't know at the time how helpful this would be. But God knew.

I know there are things in every one of your lives you would have never imagined would be true. But God knew. We didn't know when we would all be back together in this sanctuary, but God knew. "'For I know the plans that I have for you,' declares the LORD, 'plans to prosper you and not to harm you, plans to give you hope and a future'" (Jer. 29:11).

This made a big impact in my life. After I presented the message, I got an obvious sign from the Holy Spirit to finish this writing project, which can be seen as a test of faith in itself. It is a way to share my faith walk with others. When I looked at all the devotions I gave during that time (six total), they had a theme about how we communicate and connect with others. You never know what things in your life will have a big impact until you look back.

My next step was to have someone else read the book to see if I was on the right track, or at least on a track. So, after many missed opportunities to ask Pastor Scott, I finally sent the text, asking if he would read it. He agreed, and I sent the very rough draft to him. I was beyond anxious that day while I waited to see what he would say. I felt completely vulnerable because I knew it wasn't finished. The perfectionist in me was going stir crazy! I kept texting him that if it wasn't good, to just be kind in his feedback.

Fortunately, he was encouraging about the draft. Unfortunately, I knew I had a lot of work ahead of me because he would hold me accountable to finish it. It's not a bad thing to have someone else help you on your journey.

While revising, it hit me that publishing meant more than one person would read this. For a few weeks, my doubts and anxiety rose while my confidence dipped. I questioned whether I had read the sign correctly. A missed email compounded my anxiety. I thought I was being ignored, but he just didn't receive it. I had to push past my comfort zone and bring it up (not a confrontation, but it felt like it on my end!). Once we got things cleared up, I got back on track. When I did start working on the book again, my doubts declined, and my confidence started climbing.

Well, it would fluctuate, but generally, my confidence in myself grew stronger. I didn't have any experience writing something like this, but "When God calls you to do something, it isn't your job to decide if you're good enough, or if you know how to, or if it fits into the plan you have laid out for your life. It is simply your job to obey."[9] I don't know where this book will lead me, but the signs have been positive, giving me a sense of peace and joy on this journey. Each time I followed a sign, I got closer to who I was and am meant to be.

Following the signs can be a challenge regardless of where you are in your life. You may be choosing a new puzzle, job, school, or church community. You may want to close your eyes or jump off the road when it gets too scary. Getting off the path is understandable, but it's important to make sure you get back on it. I chose to go to church again because I knew I needed it, not because I felt like I had to go. I also found a church that was best for me to thrive. We are not alone on this journey of life. We have others to encourage us along the way. When making decisions about which path to take or when you need help interpreting a sign, it's always best to look to God. You can also seek help in discerning from others, like a trusted friend or pastor. I have found that when I feel peace about a decision, it's a message from God that it is right. Like Priscilla wrote, "Despite the challenges ahead of you or the naysayers around you, His voice will cause you to feel anchored by a solid sense of calm about the task He is sending you to perform."[10] When you get to your destination or

---

9 So You're a Pastor's Wife (@soyoureapastorswife), "When God calls you to do something," Facebook, June 3, 2020, https://www.facebook.com/soyoureapastorswife/posts/256112104817820.

10 Priscilla Shirer, *Discerning the Voice of God*, p. 124.

finish a project, you can look back at how you decided to follow the signs given by God or not and who helped you along the way. If you use God as your GPS, you will not be steered wrong.

- *What positive signs of faith have you followed?*
- *What are the ways you can get more involved in your church or find the right one?*
- *What was a sign you couldn't ignore that had a big impact on you?*

BUILD YOUR RESOURCE BOX

"And we know that in all things God works for the good of those who love him, who have been called according to his purpose."

(ROM. 8:28)

The next thing to decide is whether or not to use the box cover to figure out where the puzzle pieces go. Using the picture on the box is one way to use the resources you have been given to solve the problem. In life, what you have learned influences your decision-making and has molded you into who you are today. Everything you learn can become pieces in your resource box that you can use when the need arises. How have you turned what you have learned to become your resource pieces?

One example is from when I was in eighth grade. Most of my class cheated on an English test. I could have used the answers to the test as they did, but I decided to do what was right instead. As I watched my classmates cheat all around me, I knew I would not join them. It was never a question for me. I then told my mom, who let the school know. As my classmates tried to figure out who told, it became clear who didn't cheat and, therefore, who was most likely the culprit. The rest of the school year, I sat in front of a girl who kept whispering, "I know you're the one who told." I knew I couldn't react in any way because I didn't know what would happen if they found out it was me. That was the hard part of the test. One thing I remember from that time is praying. Praying that I didn't understand why I was going through all of this, but that I was going to trust in God. That was a big prayer for a young teenager. It gave me the strength and, eventually, the peace to endure. In these prayers, I feel that I was seeing the bigger picture for my life and what were important resource pieces in my box, such as honesty and integrity.

You also may not know who is watching how you handle yourself through these tests and what others may learn from you. My original eighth-grade teacher, Mrs. Laiolo, passed away during that school year. She had requested an award be given to two students who exemplified qualities that were important to her: an appreciation for learning, enthusiasm, integrity, responsibility, a sense of humor, and at least a slight fondness for chocolate (my favorite one!). To my surprise, I received this award. This gave me peace that I had done something right, even though it was hard. I put that experience in my resource box. Other people watch not only what you say but what you do in challenging moments.

Another challenging moment was when I was working with homeless families trying to get back on their feet. I worked in the children's department, watching the kids while the parents attended their classes. Some families had the Department of Social Services involved. One story that stuck out involved a little boy no older than three. I had watched him several times, and he trusted me. In one instance, I took care of him right after seeing his caseworker. This was the same caseworker who had taken him from his mom the last time he saw her. So, after his mom left, he fell apart. Usually, I could distract him with his favorite toy, a Power Ranger, but even that didn't work. He was convinced his mom was gone forever. It was horrible to watch him become more and more despondent. It was a long hour, and even when I told him I could see his mom walking towards us, he still didn't believe me. I don't know how long it took him to trust that he would not be separated from her. I learned that no matter how hard I tried to share my peace with him, he had to find his own peace within. No matter how much you want to give another person the answers, he or she needs to find them for themselves. Even though I wish I could've done more for him that day, I did my best (another piece in the box). All you can do is your best with the skills you have at the time.

One place you can obtain more skills and resources for your box is higher education, which can help you choose a career. For me, this included getting two college degrees, a bachelor's and a master's in social work. I chose social work because I wanted to help people. My first class was a diversity class. Every group we studied, I thought, yes, that's who I want to help. Then the next one. No, that's the group, and so it went. The main lesson I learned that semester was that I could help others in many ways. Then, in graduate school, I used the skills I already had and pushed myself to learn new ones to add to my resource box. Since I was in an Advanced Standing Program, I got to skip the first year of graduate school because I completed my undergraduate degree in social work. This particular school was on the quarter system, so I technically got my master's in eleven months.

Even though I completed all the coursework and field placement hours, I struggled with my self-confidence. This was one test I couldn't cheat on. I have always been a good student, but I needed to build up the self-confidence and self-esteem pieces in my box. My low confidence affected my professional performance. I needed to work through these struggles, or I wouldn't finish graduate school. A therapist helped me build confidence in myself in a few sessions. Afterward, I was better able to separate my personal struggles from my professional life. I had to dig deep into my resource box to find the strength and courage to get through it. I am grateful I sought help when I couldn't do it on my own. It may take someone helping you secure a particular piece in your resource box, and that's okay. We can all use help from others.

Even though I may not be using my MSW, I am able to take my self-confidence with me to all areas of my life. Fortunately, the skills and knowledge I obtained in both undergraduate and graduate classes are useful in many jobs and situations, including conflict resolution, mediation, empathy, and listening. I do have a passion for working with the elderly and have had a couple of jobs and two internships working directly with seniors. Unfortunately, there were other circumstances that inhibited my ability to do what I loved, including poor management practices. In stepping away from those jobs, I chose my own peace. There are many other ways I can still help the elderly, such as through the church. I have worked with people of all ages, and each job has taught me new skills and life lessons that are now in my box.

You can also obtain important resources by studying the Bible and growing your relationship with Jesus. The more time you spend learning, the more resources you can store in your box for when you need them. These resources are helpful when sharing your faith story with others. I often feel like I should have it all together before I share my story, but this is just an excuse not to do it. We all have weaknesses, but we can be strong in Christ. "I can do all this through him who gives me strength" (Phil. 4:13). The challenge is to push ourselves to share, regardless of our faults and weaknesses. We can help others add to their resource boxes by what we share in words and actions.

Unlike puzzles, we can adjust what our picture looks like during our lives. Our priorities and interests can change over time, but we can take our resource boxes with us. It can be difficult to work hard in a certain area only to discover that it's not what you want anymore. Or it might be a test to see how much you want a job in a certain field or to keep a certain relationship. I am here to say that it's okay if you change what your personal puzzle looks like. You have a unique place to be, and the journey is to figure out where you are meant to be. As Christine Caine wrote, "I fully believe that God has given each of you a specific purpose and destiny (Ps. 138:8). YOU are a God-ordained puzzle piece that fits perfectly into His strategy for reaching the hurting and lost at this very moment in time."[11]

---

11 Christine Caine, @christinecaine, "I fully believe that God has given each of you," Facebook, January 16, 2019, https://www.facebook.com/permalink.php?story_fbid=101614783432900 89&id=143678730088.

I have to admit that I use the box cover when putting together a puzzle. But unlike a puzzle, you don't get your life's full picture in the beginning. You slowly piece it together until the picture becomes clearer and clearer. Having the picture on the box is like wanting the answers before the test, whatever the test might be. Just remember that you are building your resource box every day to prepare you for whatever challenge or test is ahead. God will use those challenges for good. And no, I wouldn't consider looking at the box cover as cheating.

- *What are the most important resource pieces in your box?*
- *What was your hardest test, and what did you learn by going through it?*
- *What are your weaknesses, and how can you strengthen them using your faith?*

SET AND BREAK BOUNDARIES

*"Now may the Lord of peace himself give you peace
at all times and in every way."*

(2 THESS. 3:16)

Once you decide on a puzzle and have gathered all the resources (pieces), the fun of putting it together begins. Most people start with the edge pieces (aka the boundaries) to see what the full size of the puzzle will look like. Likewise, you need boundaries in your life so you can see what the limits are. For example, edges of the road, cliffs, fences, personal space, and socially acceptable behaviors are all part of everyday life. Our current dogs, Shadow and Pasha, have taught me many lessons about boundaries.

The first lesson is you need to figure out what your boundaries are so you'll know if you have crossed them. We have a gate at our house we have to open and close to pull our vehicles into the driveway. Our dogs watch us as we open it and usually respect the invisible line. One time, Shadow saw a cat across the street and took off running towards it. I don't think she realized she had run across the street and stopped at the neighbor's fence. She thought she was okay because she stopped at a fence. Unfortunately, it was the wrong one. She had gone too far. Isn't that true about us? We sometimes don't realize we have gone too far until it's too late. What happens when you break a boundary? Depending on what the boundary was, it can be a rough road ahead. This is where faith and asking for forgiveness comes in. Then you can reset that boundary and have peace.

The second lesson is sometimes you have to expand your boundaries or extend the edges to make the pieces fit. Our other dog, Pasha, broke our boundary soon after she came to live with us. I planned on going on a short walk in our neighborhood and was trying to get the dogs to cooperate long enough to get their harnesses on. Shadow cooperated, but Pasha was resistant, so I told her, "Fine, I'm going without you." Once Shadow and I were outside the fence, Pasha wasn't happy we were leaving without her. She jumped the fence and came running. Luckily, my husband saw this, grabbed her leash, and came running behind. I looked behind me and saw a dog running at us—I was relieved it was my own dog. She came right to me, and I could loop the leash through her collar until Jeffrey got there. Sometimes, a temporary boundary can help you be more willing to cooperate.

Unfortunately, once Pasha figured out she could make it over the fence, the temptation to jump over again overtook our desire for her to stay in the yard. I'm sure we have all done things to test boundaries, like staying out past curfew or driving above the speed limit. I can be the first to admit I have done both, and once I had done it, it was easier to rationalize doing it again. Pushing those boundaries can be a slippery slope once they have been broken. While I was grounded for breaking curfew, the threat of punishment didn't stop me from breaking that boundary again. Hopefully, you can learn from getting in trouble for breaking God's boundaries. You can also learn from the first example in the Bible: Adam and Eve. They were given an opportunity to break or keep the one boundary God had given them. They had access to all the fruits from all the trees, except one, and the temptation was too great. By giving in to their temptation, they were kicked out of Eden. Personal and biblical lessons can remind us to stay within the boundaries we are given.

Luckily, Pasha would stay close by and come back when called. What's funny is she could have jumped back in without us knowing, but she was too busy with her freedom. Isn't that also true of us? We could get ourselves back inside the boundaries, but we often become stubborn. Pasha could have just decided to cooperate in the first place and come on the walk, but she wanted to do it her way. Stubborn again. We extended our fence so she couldn't continue breaking the boundary. You may learn that you need to raise a boundary to ensure you can maintain it for yourself with Christ's help.

It's important to remember that most boundaries are there to protect us from harm, which leads me to the third lesson: we set boundaries for everyone's safety. When we take our dogs for a walk, we always put on their harnesses. So, when we pass other dogs, we know we have control over ours. Our dogs are friendly, but we know they will go into protection mode if they feel threatened. On one walk, a dog ran out of his yard and came towards us. Our dogs tried to get in front of us as we tried to maneuver them away. Once the dog's owner came out to help, we were able to get them separated. Everyone could then return to a state of peace and harmony. Because we had our boundary, we were able to keep everyone safe.

You don't always know what boundaries other people have. This can cause awkward situations. For example, if someone isn't comfortable giving hugs greets a hugger, the hugger might unknowingly cross the other person's boundary. This boundary may have been caused by something traumatic in their past. The hugger may unintentionally have triggered the non-hugger. Or maybe they are just uncomfortable with hugs. We must learn how to respect other people's feelings about personal space. We have taught our dogs to sit, put their front paws on our shoulders, and give us a hug. There have been many times I have asked for a hug from one of them, and they just walk away or don't make eye contact. If I keep pushing, they bark at me to tell me to leave them alone. You have to be aware of the other person's verbal and nonverbal communication and respect his or her space. It's important to respect what makes both people feel comfortable and safe.

The fourth lesson is to watch for stumbling blocks (mental, physical, or spiritual) when you start moving past a boundary or over the edge. If you're not paying attention, you can fall into bad habits, addiction, and sin. Or, as in one of my clumsy moments, actually falling. One night, as I walked down the stairs in our house, like I have done a thousand times before, I didn't turn the light on because I knew where I was going. What I didn't know was Shadow was sprawled on the second step, as she had also done a thousand times before. Well, the combination of darkness and an almost all-black dog created a stumbling block for me. I went to step down and realized she was there. I tried to stop myself from stepping on her and stepped on air instead, then tumbled down the final two steps. Don't worry, the tile floor and wall stopped my momentum, but not before I slammed my left knee into the floor. Ouch! I hobbled back upstairs after a few seconds of shock. Thankfully, it was just a bad bruise and a constant reminder for several days as I hobbled around. When we told some friends about my tumble, they went out and bought us some nightlights. They helped give me some light, even when I was stubbornly staying in the dark. The same thing can be applied spiritually. If we remain in darkness and refuse to see the light in Jesus, we'll keep going down the wrong path and stay outside the boundary. So, be aware of your surroundings and make sure the light of Jesus is leading you. "Turn from evil and do good; seek peace and pursue it" (Ps. 34:14).

The other side of putting up boundaries is when you stop yourself from doing something because you don't think you can, which is the fifth lesson. Sometimes you need to take small steps when trying something new. While out on walks, we like to get the dogs in the water if possible. Our dogs are lab mixes, so you would think they would jump right in, but you would be wrong. We had to start small. We started by taking them to the water's edge and giving them lots of encouragement. Once Pasha started walking a little in the water, Shadow tried it also. After doing this several times, I wanted to see if they would get in deeper water. One camping trip, I tried walking out in the water with them. One would come out a few feet but then quickly go back to shore. Then the other would venture out a little and do the same thing. It was funny how they thought they could jump out of the water and not land back in it. Jeffrey was on the shore to cheer them on and be there as their safe base. You have people in your life standing either in the water or on the shore, cheering you on as you try something new. I don't think we'll ever get the dogs to swim, but they did push their boundaries and try something new. You don't have to limit yourself to only things you have done before.

You can also limit what God can do when you limit yourself. There have been so many times when I thought I couldn't do something, but I took a chance and cooperated. This can apply to all areas of your life—jobs/careers, leading a specific committee, public speaking, or fill in the blank. When I started the job as a caregiver, I had thought I would be okay working in the office down the line, as long as I didn't have to do scheduling. Well, God probably had a good laugh because guess what, that's what I was asked to do: scheduling. Not only that, I actually excelled at it. You never know if you are going to be good at something unless you give it a chance. Yes, sometimes it's not something you're good at or like, but at least you have tried to push yourself outside that comfort zone. You can find peace in knowing you have tried.

The Bible has many more examples of boundaries I encourage you to find. Priscilla Shirer writes, "Scripture is the primary way God speaks, and it provides the boundaries into which everything He says will fall."[12] If you feel uneasy (lacking peace) about whether you are getting close to breaking a boundary, you might be. When any questions arise about a boundary, go to the Word and prayer. Most boundaries are set for your safety, but some are meant to be broken, like trying something new.

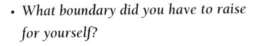

- *What boundary did you have to raise for yourself?*
- *What has been a stumbling block for you, and how can you seek God when you recognize one?*
- *When have you limited God by limiting yourself?*

---

12 Priscilla Shirer, *Discerning the Voice of God*, p. 86.

FIVE

TO CONTROL OR NOT CONTROL

"Faith is something that God gives you that you use and release in your life."[13]

Now that you have your boundaries established, it is time to start filling in all the other pieces. When I put a puzzle together, my next step is sorting the pieces by color. It helps me categorize each section and tackle smaller parts at a time. One piece doesn't make sense until it starts connecting with other pieces. These smaller finished sections, or parts of your life, can make you feel

13 Joyce Meyer, *Galatians Bible Study—Part 1*, January 7, 2019, https://joycemeyer.org/todaysshow/2019/02/galatians-bible-study-part-1, video.

like you have some sense of control, especially when you look at the whole puzzle. It can also give you a feeling of accomplishment as the puzzle (your life) starts to take shape, which often encourages you to keep going. But what if you put more trust in God rather than trying to control all aspects of your life?

The desire to control can be seen in various parts of your life. Two common areas are when you learn to ride a bike and drive a car. Both require control in steering and speed. When riding a bike, most people start with training wheels. Then, when you feel you have enough control, the training wheels come off, and you try to pedal, balance, and steer. In most cases, someone helps you, which becomes an area of trust (relinquishing control). You must trust them to know when to let go. You can apply this to your faith: "You can have faith or you can have control, but you can't have both."[14] You have to be able to give God control to show you have faith. It is easy to say but hard to actually do. Thank goodness that God will never let go of us, even when we think we can handle something on our own!

The need for control is even more apparent when you learn to drive. It can be scary to get behind the driver's seat for the first time. It can be just as scary for the instructor, maybe even more so, because they are not in control (and want to show you that they have faith in you). My first driving lesson was in an empty parking lot with my dad. Then, I had a lesson with a paid instructor, where I had to get on the freeway in California. My training wheels were taken off much quicker than I would have liked. However, I can see that it was good for me to get that first experience under my belt because it gave me confidence. Driving shows us that we can

---

14 Craig Groeshel, (@craiggroeshel), "You can have faith," Instagram, April 10, 2021, https://www.instagram.com/p/CNflsgqAwAJ/?utm_source=ig_web_copy_link.

only control ourselves. We have to react to what other drivers are doing, but we only have the power to control our own actions. "You don't always have the power to control, but you do always have the power to surrender."[15] When you can see, or better yet trust without seeing, that God's ways are better than yours, there is peace in surrendering control.

More recently, we bought an ATV. My husband is the driver, and I am the passenger. At first, it was scary not to be in control, and I had to trust that my husband would steer us properly and stay on the path. I wanted to jump off a few times, but like riding a bike or getting on the freeway the first time, I pushed past my fear. I had to learn to lean into the driver to help us get up the hill and not work against him. We also see that, when empowered, we can accomplish many things when we push past our fears and start to trust. God wants you to push past any fears and lean into him as your driver. He can give us freedom from whatever has control over us if we trust him. With that surrender comes joy and peace.

The desire to control can even come into play when we read the Bible and pray. You decide how much time you want to spend and whether or not you are open to listening. A few years back, I had challenged myself to read the whole Bible in one year. My main focus should have been to learn, but it felt more like I was simply marking off each verse, chapter, and book as I read. I learned things I didn't know before, but it was too much to read and understand in just 365 days. My motivation was skewed in that I finished the section, but I wasn't always taking the time to listen for what God wanted to show me that day. I

---

15 Alan George, (@alanvgeorge), "You don't have the power," Instagram, April 10, 2021, https://www.instagram.com/p/CLekjttB46f/?utm_source=ig_web_copy_link.

learned to put the focus back on learning and let God be in control during my study and prayer time. God gave me another lesson during this Bible reading challenge. It was an evening when I was taking work calls at home. I was working on replacing a caregiver at a shift for the next day. It was a challenge because the client lived out of town, and not all the caregivers were willing to drive that far for just a couple of hours. I decided to take a break from making calls and sat down for my readings. On this day, I read Matthew 6, which ends in: "Therefore do not worry about tomorrow, for tomorrow will worry about itself. Each day has enough trouble of its own" (verse 34). I took that hint to hand over the control to God, knowing it would be okay. We can all be more open to hearing those hints to trust as we pray and read the Bible. These moments can help you let go of control and trust God in all areas of your life.

Scheduling was a delicate balance of control between the caregivers and clients. I wanted to keep everyone happy, which was challenging. I thought of scheduling as putting pieces together to make everything run smoothly. All the clients having a caregiver to assist them was a successful day. Sometimes it took some shuffling around, adjusting times, and switching caregivers to make it all work. There were times when it was only by the grace of God that we got it all figured out because certain clients had so many restrictions about who could go to their homes. There were other times when what I thought was the best plan didn't work out. Sometimes, it took more time for me to figure it out, but in the end, it was a success. The client was happy, but I have to admit that was more of God's work than mine. Most calls I made to clients were bad news. It meant I needed to adjust their time, there would be a different caregiver, or someone was quitting. I remember telling them several times that if I had the power to control other people, my job would be a lot easier.

Even though I felt in control, a lot of the time, that job controlled me. Even when I wasn't at work, I was checking my work phone for messages or logging in to see if everyone made it to their shifts. There were many times I even checked my work phone while in a Bible study class or Sunday service. It was a weird transition when I quit and went from scheduling everyone else's lives to having no schedule for myself. My mind had always been thinking about how to cover a shift or who could be another option or wondering if it was all running smoothly. When I quit and turned in the phone, that responsibility left me, and peace came in. It was like letting God do what only he can do. Putting that into practice is hard, yet he reminds us over and over that it is imperative and shows our trust and faith in him.

I find it intriguing that the job I accepted several weeks after quitting the home care job was as a receptionist in a medical office. The ironic part is that I am still scheduling but in a more limited way. A person needs to make an appointment, and I offer an available time when the doctor will be in the office. I don't have to manipulate the doctor's schedule to make it work for the patient. I also can leave work at work, which shows me that this job doesn't control me as the previous one did. It is important to have this separation, if possible, for a good work-life balance.

Only a few weeks into this job, I offered to help with the billing piece of the business. I had done billing at other jobs, so it seemed natural to me. To have success in billing, you need all the pieces to fit together just right. First, you make sure everything is entered correctly into the system, which requires cooperation from the patient. If just one piece isn't right, the insurance claim is denied.

Trying to figure out what may have been entered incorrectly and how to correct it to resubmit can feel like solving a complicated puzzle. Payments also need to be properly entered to complete a patient's visit in the system. When one of those hard claims is paid, I celebrate, like when I successfully filled a shift at my old job. The desire to finish that claim took time, putting the work in, and sometimes patient cooperation, but it is the joy and peace that comes out of it that makes it worth it. Fortunately for us, when we decide to let God into our lives, he makes it all worth it in the end.

In all these examples, it was hard to give up the control to someone else: a family member, clients, caregivers, and especially, God. This is where you want to cling to control the most, but time and time again, he reminds you that you are not in control. I've heard it often said to tell God your plans but do it in pencil. Many years ago, I wrote the following about control: "I make sure I volunteer because I know it'll get done. Otherwise, even though people are nice, things may not get done."[16] As you can see, this is an ongoing struggle for me. I imagine it is for others as well, even if it looks different. It is impossible to control everything around you. All it does is wear you down, which is why we all have to be more willing to put our trust in God. Even if it is scary to let go, giving God control is crucial to receiving peace.

So, no matter what you're working on, whether it's reading the Bible, breaking down tasks to complete at work, or trying something new, it's important to remember all you can do is take on one thing at a time. And it's okay to give God control. "Anything under God's control is never out of control."[17]

---

16 Rebecca Nolting. Journal entry. March 5, 2002.

17 Akash Naik, https://www.123rf.com/photo_121471114_inspirational-quotes-anything-under-god-s-control-is-never-out-of-control-positive-motivational.html.

- *What area(s) in your life do you keep tight control over? Do you try to control your study and prayer time?*
- *How does your level of control affect your decision-making?*
- *Where can you try to let go of some control?*

DISCOVER YOUR UNIQUE PIECES

*"There's nothing more exciting than being
the person God created you to be. Strange as
you might be, be yourself."*[18]

Once you sort the pieces, you can start trying to see where they
go. Often the joy of solving a puzzle comes from finding the right
fit after countless tries. We are all searching for where we fit into
the bigger puzzle of life, but first, we have to figure out what our
own pieces look like that make each of us unique. These choices

---

18 Joyce Meyer, Living Courageously Sermon from *Enjoying Everyday Life*, aired early 2019.

can be challenging if you worry about what other people think, even if they are not what society deems as "normal." A few things that make you unique relate to your home: where you live, who you choose as a partner, and what your family looks like.

Your first unique piece is the time and place you were born. One of my favorite books of the Bible is Esther. Her story is unique because she was chosen to marry the Persian king, even though she was secretly Jewish. She used her position as queen to save the lives of the Jewish people. She chose to stand up for what she knew was right, even with the risk of being killed herself, and helped a lot of people. It's one of my favorites because she is a great role model for taking on a challenge. It gives me hope and confidence that I can take on challenges with God's help. Esther was, as we say, "in the right place at the right time," or you could say that God put her there for that reason. One of the repeating verses is "for such a time as this" (Esther 4:14). It reminds me that there is a reason we are where and when we are. There was and is a plan for us, as it says in Isaiah:

> "Lord, you are my God;
> I will exalt you and praise your name,
> for in perfect faithfulness
> you have done wonderful things,
> things planned long ago." (Isa. 25:1)

The places you have lived make you unique. People have asked me, "How did you go from living in California to Pueblo, Colorado?" I would tell them about going to graduate school and meeting my husband, but the true answer is "God." Who else would have planned and known the places I would choose? Growing up,

I listened to a lot of country music, like Reba McEntire, Kenny Rogers, and Dolly Parton. My oldest sister introduced me to newer country singers (at that time) like Shania Twain and Garth Brooks. One of the things I looked forward to when I got old enough was to go line dancing. I went country dancing a few times while living in Sacramento, so I looked for a place when I moved to Denver. This was where I met Jeffrey, who knew how to two-step, and took the leap to move to Pueblo. I had never even heard of Pueblo before moving to Colorado, but I couldn't imagine being anywhere else.

Let me two-step back to how I met my husband. When I moved to Denver, I decided I wanted to just meet new people and have fun. For Christmas, one of my friends gave me an interesting gift—an address book. She challenged me to get phone numbers from guys for each letter of the alphabet. I accepted the challenge and recruited a friend to help me. We had a specific strategy: we would find two or more males (no females) and alternate who would ask them to dance. If we liked them, we would stay to visit. If they said they didn't know how to dance, we would try to teach them. It was a win-win. Well, Jeffrey came one night with a couple of male friends, and we hung out with them for a bit. He was the only one out of the three who really knew how to country dance. We got their numbers added to the book. They started regularly coming on Saturday nights, and Jeffrey was allowed to have my phone number as well. After a couple of months of getting to know each other, we started dating, and he danced his way into my heart. It could have only been God who would use a silly challenge like that to bring us together.

Couples often discuss their dreams for the future, including any plans for children. My dreams growing up were "normal"— have a career, get married, and have kids. I babysat for neighbors and family friends and had a few jobs working with youth. Even though I enjoyed being around kids, I suppose I never felt that maternal instinct many women have. I think I figured that when it was time, I would be ready. I remember telling my mom on a few occasions, "If I had kids, I would do [blank] differently." It was an if, not a when.

My family puzzle piece looks different from what I had imagined it would look like. When I was living in Denver, I don't remember exactly when it happened, but I remember hearing a whisper from God saying, "It's okay not to have kids." What I find interesting was it wasn't "don't have kids," but that it was okay if I didn't. Not feeling the pressure to follow the "normal" path gave me a feeling of peace. You may think it was a snap decision. However, I was going through some of my other writings soon after that moment of pure peace when I found a list of 101 traits I was looking for in a husband. (I now wish I had kept it, but I can say I never used it.) The one that jumped out to me was: "Ok with not having kids or adopting." I wrote this list when I was eighteen, many years before that whisper. I believe this was from God because, as Priscilla said, "When He speaks to you internally and then causes other events to confirm what He's saying, it's not coincidence, luck, or chance. It is likely His sovereign hand orchestrating circumstances to help lead you to His will. When God speaks, he does so persistently."[19] I was meant to keep that list to help confirm this decision. While I wasn't active in church at that time, God was still reaching out to me. "Peace is not only an element of His character, but it is also evidence of His presence."[20] Even though I heard a whisper, I still had the choice to decide

---

19 Priscilla Shirer, *Discerning the Voice of God*, p. 76.
20 Priscilla Shirer, *Discerning the Voice of God*, p. 124.

whether I would have kids or not. Having a choice was at the root of the peace I felt. God gave me the choice, but I had to choose to accept it.

Once I made that decision, I knew the next step of faith would be telling other people. There were times I was tempted to just go along with everyone else. I wanted to fit in and knew if I didn't have children, then I wouldn't have that shared experience with others. Thankfully, I knew in my heart where the peace was, which gave me the strength to consciously confirm my decision over and over. People tried to convince me to change my mind, saying I would regret it. Since I wasn't active in the church at that time, I felt uncomfortable explaining this moment of pure peace. Actually, I think this is the first time I have shared this very personal moment. Many people have probably made assumptions about why I don't have children, from being focused on my career to fertility issues to being selfish to who knows what. For those with whom I have discussed this, they have asked if I regret this decision, and I can honestly say, "No." Do I enjoy spending time with nieces and nephews and other kids? Sure. Have I had moments when I wonder what it would have been like if I had made a different decision? Sure. But do I perceive that I am missing a piece in my puzzle? No. I think it meant I could serve God in my own unique way. "Focus on being yourself. God made you to be different."[21]

I have also heard many times you don't know what unconditional love is until you have children. While I can respect their opinion, I know I have felt unconditional love when taking care of others and my dogs. I can also choose to give my love to those

---

21 Chrystal Evans Hurst, "You Were Made to Be Different," January 31, 2019, https://proverbs31.org/read/devotions/full-post/2019/01/31/you-were-made-to-be-different, accessed May 9, 2021.

in my life—at work, at church, with family and friends and even strangers. You also have that choice.

One thing I haven't mentioned about my husband is that he's nineteen years older than me. The age gap is often easily misunderstood in our culture, partly because it is uncommon. This was never an issue for him or me. Because of his age, many people have assumed it was just his decision not to have kids, which is a wrong assumption. We both had made the decision before we met and then confirmed the decision together. Naturally, people in our lives wondered about our age difference in the beginning. For example, they thought I was looking for a sugar daddy or was just a trophy girlfriend. It took time and faith for our loved ones to accept and embrace our relationship. The large age difference may not be as common, but we both choose to make our relationship work, and that's what matters. The spouse piece has made my puzzle more complete.

One of the bigger challenges to our relationship was from my mother-in-law. She struggled to accept all her children's significant others, not just ours. Those siblings who had been through it before us gave us advice on how to handle the situation. Their main advice was to make our own choices without worrying about making her happy. My mother-in-law eventually accepted me. I let go of how I was treated in the past and even sat with her in the hospital after she broke her hip, which gave me needed peace. I can now look at this as a time where grace won.

God can speak to us in many ways, including through people we meet. It isn't a coincidence that they spoke to you during a specific moment in time. Once the puzzle pieces start coming together, you can see that you are where you're supposed to be "for such a time as this" (Esther 4:14) in your own unique way.

- *What areas, if any, in your life have you felt like you were not following the "norm"? How did this strengthen your faith?*

- *How has God called you to be different?*

- *How can you be more like Esther and stand up for something, even if there is a risk?*

CAN A WRONG PIECE TURN INTO A RIGHT ONE?

"God has a perfect plan for the things we deem good,
but also what we perceive as difficult."[22]

During the trial-and-error phase, you probably try more wrong than right pieces, ones that don't quite fit. It can be frustrating not to get them in the right spot on the first try. That piece then goes back into the pile, rejected for that particular spot. Then there are times when you think you have the piece placed correctly, but then discover it's wrong. You may think that piece

---

22 Kia Stephens, @kianstephens, "God has a perfect plan for all things," Instagram, December 11, 2020, https://www.instagram.com/p/ClpjbmiA613/?utm_source=ig_web_copy_link.

doesn't fit in your puzzle, or you don't want it to be there. These unexpected pieces can challenge us to grow in ways we wouldn't have otherwise.

One of the pieces I wasn't planning for was a minor car accident. It was an in-the-wrong-place-at-the-wrong-time moment. Or was it? The girl who hit my car didn't see me until it was too late. Both of our cars had only minor damage, but it was enough of an impact to cause lower back strain. I was still able to do most things, like work, but with minor modifications. I was thankful that this was my only injury. Unlike my other accidents, where I only have minimal memories, I can recall every piece of this accident, which was a detriment to me mentally. At first, I played the "what if" game. We have all played that game with situations in our lives. Mine included: what if I had just been going a little faster so she wouldn't have hit me, what if I hadn't been on that road at that time, or what if I hadn't tensed up when she hit me (which is what caused the back strain)? I also could take that game the other way: what if she had hit me harder to make my car spin, what if other cars had been closer and hit us too, or what if I had more serious injuries?

Since I have a clear memory of what happened, I am more acutely aware of vehicles coming too close to me. When they start to pull out, I am ready to react. Right after the accident, I had to drive home and then to the police station a couple of hours later to file the report. I am grateful for this immediate need to literally get back in the driver's seat so that fear didn't have time to paralyze me from driving. It can be tempting to just give something up, so you don't have that chance of being hurt again. Even if you feel like that rejected piece put back in the box, it's important not to let fear drive your future decisions.

As much as I wish that this unexpected piece wasn't part of my puzzle, I am thankful for it. I feel I have gotten stronger mentally and physically, but it has taken time and work. My chiropractor gave me a series of stretches and encouraged me to walk more. It was tempting to just ignore them. I downplayed their importance as my back started to feel better. Unfortunately, or maybe fortunately, my back pain increased again, and I needed to take the healing process more seriously if I truly wanted total healing. This included letting go of blaming myself for the accident. Yes, another person was responsible, and I was never angry at her for hitting me, but I was feeling the effects of this added stress. It was stressful dealing with the insurance company and getting my car repaired, which affected my healing. I have this quote on my fridge that I got several years ago at a meeting: "Allow your friend to make mistakes and give yourself the same freedom."[23] Once I let go of the self-blame and forgave myself for the accident, I was able to focus more on my healing. This can be harder than forgiving someone else, but it is so crucial to find this peace.

This piece also helped me remember activities I enjoy but hadn't made much time for. I was told to walk more, so I pulled out my Walkman and started making more of an effort to go on walks. The more I walked, the better I felt, and my motivation increased to keep going. I used to go on walks when I was younger, and it helped clear my mind. Besides forgiving myself, this act of self-care has been a blessing. It is so easy not to prioritize taking care of yourself. Remember, you're with yourself all the time, no matter who else is around. On one of my walks, I had this thought: Loving others includes loving and taking care

23 Anonymous.

of yourself. Only God could take what I had viewed as a wrong piece and turn it into a right one.

Besides walking, I was reminded of how much joy I feel when I write. I had given myself a deadline for this writing project and was pushing myself to meet it. This accident gave me a setback on writing too. Not only was it uncomfortable to sit for longer than a few minutes, but I also had no motivation to write. Each of these chapters had me reflecting on my past, which could be painful. My deadline added stress, which also affected my healing process. I had to let go of my self-imposed deadline and focus on healing. This unexpected piece has taught me a lot more than I bargained for, or as a quote I found said, "In short, don't let that strain in your back become a strain on your life."[24] Once I got stronger mentally and physically, the inspiration to write came back. Putting self-care as a top priority is vital to our physical and mental health.

Another thing that I learned is that even if you think you have things planned out, there will always be curveballs. I definitely prefer to have everything organized, set plans ahead of time, and be prepared for any meeting or event. But "God will let you walk into uncomfortable situations where all you can do is rely on Him. Don't be anxious. He's about to show you He is faithful."[25] There are many people in the Bible that were thrown curveballs, so I know I'm not alone in this, and neither are you. We just need to learn how to adapt to these perceived wrong or unexpected pieces.

---

24 Cottage Health, "Back Strains and Sprains," July 3, 2018, https://www.cottagehealth.org/about/newsroom/2018/understanding-back-strains-and-sprains/, accessed May 9, 2021.

25 Women of Faith, @womenoffaith, "God will let you walk into uncomfortable situations," Instagram, August 29, 2020, https://www.instagram.com/p/CEfTydDgPkn/?utm_source=ig_web_copy_link.

This accident has made me more vulnerable because, like my damaged car, others have seen my imperfections. First, others could see the damaged section before the car was repaired. Since it was repaired, no one can tell its past. Actually, it looks even better since the back bumper had other previous damage, and now it looks like new. Before the insurance company agreed to repair my car, they had to determine if it was considered a total loss. Fortunately, even though it was close, they agreed to fix it. You can also apply this analogy to people. You can look at someone's past and see only the damages. Thankfully, God sees past all our damages, physically and mentally, and loves us anyway. Everyone has pieces in their past they would like to pretend were not part of their puzzle, but many of these wrong or unexpected pieces have helped steer us in the right direction and made things better than they were before.

Second, even though my injury was not obvious, it showed my health isn't perfect either. I am healthy overall, but my healing took longer because my chiropractor told me I was "deconditioned." This meant that because I hadn't been exercising like I should have been in recent years, my body took longer to heal. This extended healing time was frustrating and motivating at the same time. In addition to forgiving myself, I had to give myself grace in this process. I can't change the past, but I can try to do better in the future, which gives me a sense of peace. I am coming out of this experience stronger than I was before and can place this piece in its rightful spot in my puzzle.

Our perceived wrong pieces can test our faith walk. You want to look like the "perfect Christian," but there's no such thing. My mom and I joke about being perfect, finding a perfect greeting card, or cooking a good meal. When I was a child, my mom said something about being perfect, and I told her, "Only God was perfect." The Book of Hebrews has several references to this fact. We are made perfect through our relationship with Jesus. I found this post that describes this difference so well:

"Perfectionism
It's all about me
It's about what I do
If I obey, then God will love me
I am always trying to win God's approval

Grace
It's about Jesus
It's about what Jesus already did
Because God loves me, I can obey
I am living from God's approval."[26]

One area I struggle to obey is praying aloud without any preparation ahead of time. I want it to sound just right, but that's my worry, not God's. When you feel like you are refusing to let those "wrong" pieces fit into your puzzle or feeling the pressure to appear perfect in front of others, this is the right time to pray. The following prayer is how I want to end this chapter. You can read it either as a prayer to forgive someone else or yourself. Let us pray:

---

26 Alan George, @alanvgeorge, "Perfectionism, It's All About Me," Instagram, November 24, 2020, https://www.instagram.com/p/CH_xEFAKvwe/?utm_source=ig_web_copy_link.

Dear Lord,

Set me free of all that binds me,

That stops me from loving people (myself) with grace.

Set me free from the expectations I have of

other people (myself)

And love them (myself) solely for who they are (I am).

Set me free from all the pain that I have felt in the past

And help me love like I've never been hurt before.

Set me free of the resentment of seeing other people succeed

And help me to just be happy for them.

Set me free of the fear of failure,

But give me the knowledge that even if I have the chance

to fail,

I also have the chance to succeed.

Also, if I do fail, I can get back up with YOUR help.

Please, Lord, guide me to wise decisions,

To keep my faith in YOU always,

And to never forget your constant presence

In faith, hope, and love. Amen.

- *What perceived wrong pieces turned into right ones?*
- *When have you let fear drive your decisions instead of peace?*
- *When was the last time you thanked God for loving you despite your past?*

LOSING AND FINDING PIECES

"Don't let people pull you into their storm…pull them into your peace."[27]

Sometimes, even if the puzzle is brand new, there can be a missing piece or two. In life, you can have a piece, or several, go missing, or maybe they can be better described as lost. These pieces can be people, personal items, or memories. You may go through the stages of grief for any or all these losses. It is also how you look at the losses. What have you learned from the person or situation that you carry with you?

---

27 Mindful Christianity, @mindfulchristianity, "Don't Let People Pull You into Their Storm," Facebook, August 9, 2019, https://www.facebook.com/MINDFULCHRISTIANITY/posts/2387604598188381.

While doing the Route 66 puzzle, I kept dropping pieces on the floor. Usually, my dogs didn't even notice. One time though, Shadow was chewing a couple of pieces before I even realized what happened. Even if I had gotten them out of her mouth, they would not have blended in well. This changed the finished product because now I had a couple of missing pieces. Even with something simple like missing puzzle pieces, I went through the stages of grief—denial (no, they're not really missing), anger (why did I let the pieces fall on the floor?), bargaining (can I salvage the pieces?), depression (now the puzzle will not be complete), and finally, acceptance (it is what it is). The acceptance stage can also be described as being at peace. I believe this is fitting for the final stage because if you have peace, what else do you truly need?

When I was nineteen, someone broke into my apartment and stole my things. It was almost surreal because I had decided to take a break from studying and went to browse at a bookstore. I then decided to walk through this little shopping area and had some of the most peaceful minutes, listening to some soft music while strolling along. I think I was led there so I would not run into the burglar. It was weird to go from that deep peace to complete chaos in only a few minutes. I saw our door open, a knife on the kitchen floor, and my stuff missing. The burglar stole a piece of my peace. I didn't know what I was walking into as I checked the entire apartment. I called for my roommates, but both were gone. I went to the apartment office, and they helped me call the police. It was a total violation of my privacy and safety. I had to work through those stages of grief. They only stole material items, but they also took my peace of mind and innocence that day. It took time to feel comfortable where I was living and trust that it was most likely a random act. They never did recover my stolen items. When I got to the stage of acceptance, I found the peace for which I was searching. I learned that even lost pieces shape who we become.

When you lose someone, it can also feel like a piece is missing. One of the pieces that helped shape me I lost when I was sixteen: my grandpa (my mom's dad). I loved all my grandparents, but I had an extra special connection with my grandpa, Jacob. When I was little, he would read me one of my favorite books, *Danny and the Dinosaur*. When my husband and I went to the Dinosaur National Monument in Utah, I had the book with me and sat down to read it. The book is about a dinosaur that escapes the museum for a day, so I figured being surrounded by dinosaur fossils was a good place to feel closer to my grandpa. While I had the book in my hands, a hand-drawn picture that my grandpa had drawn of me on a dinosaur fell out. So precious!

My grandpa and I also connected over pigs. One of his jobs was as a pig farmer—maybe that's where my collection of pig items started, or maybe it was how he said my name, Becky. His voice made it sound closer to piggy. That's at least how I remember him saying it the last time I saw him in Minnesota. He had Alzheimer's and didn't recognize us at that point, but when my mom told him who I was, he repeated it. What a beautiful moment to hear him say it that last time. His brief moment of clarity is a memory I hold dear, even though he wouldn't remember. Anyone who has had a loved one with memory loss knows it can feel like you go through the stages of grief multiple times. First, when they start forgetting things and then when they forget who their loved ones are. It's a series of losses while they are still alive, which is heartbreaking as you watch them decline. There is peace in those small moments of clarity that can sustain you.

During that last visit, a thunderstorm came through in the middle of the night, and the tornado siren started. I grew up in California, so this was an unfamiliar sound. We realized we should get to lower ground, just in case. We woke up my grandparents, who were sleeping soundly, and tried to get them to the basement. We got my grandpa a few steps down to a landing when we decided to stop there. There we all sat on the steps around four in the morning, listening to the weather updates on the radio. My grandpa looked so at peace that I think that is why I remained calm. The storm passed, and we went back upstairs. Even though he had lost his memory, he found a way to have peace and showed me how to do the same through a storm. We have all had storms or struggles that have lacked peace and can feel like we are going through it alone. You can draw strength from past storms, from God, and from others when you face the next one.

How do you remember your lost pieces after they are gone? Do you have a special item of theirs, photos, or videos? I have seen a lot of people with tattoos in remembrance of a person. I have one as well, but not like you may think. I have only one tattoo on my ankle: a flying pig. Yes, you read that right. As I said, my grandpa was a pig farmer, and I believe he's now in heaven, which is the reason for the wings. But I can also use it as a reminder to believe in the impossible, like the saying, "when pigs fly." Or as Jesus said, "With man this is impossible, but with God all things are possible" (Matt. 19:26). Even though I lost my grandpa several years ago, I found a way to remember him in a special way. I can carry this piece with me, and it gives me a sense of peace when I look at it. You can also find your own special way to remember the loved ones in your life. It doesn't have to make sense to anyone else. It is your way to stay connected.

Your ancestors have been a part of shaping you as well and learning about them can help you feel that connection with them. In 2010, my husband and I went to Germany to visit friends. We did a lot of sightseeing and experienced the German culture, but the best day was when we drove to a small town to try and find where my ancestors had lived. My mom's family had done some tracing years before, so I had something to go on: go to the town of Mittelehrenbach and ask for the Heim house (our family name). Fortunately, our friend was from Germany and helped us translate because my memory from high school German wasn't going to cut it. We found the Heim house and knocked on the door. An older gentleman answered and welcomed us in when we explained I might be related to him. When I had our friend ask if he remembered meeting my aunt and uncle years before, he told me I looked like his sister. I never quite figured out how we were officially related, but it doesn't really matter. Family is family. He offered to take us to the cemetery where his other relatives were buried (I guess mine too!). I still have a walnut from the tree on his property. We all want to have a moment like that. We are all God's creation and part of his family. This connection to my past gave me a peace I didn't know I was missing until I found it.

Missing (aka lost) pieces can also be found in the Bible. There are a few stories in a row in Luke 15 about people who lost something—first a sheep, then a coin, and finally, a son, or more familiarly, the prodigal son. All the stories revolve around searching for the lost and rejoicing when it is found. It didn't matter that they had other sheep, other coins, or even another son. What mattered is they noticed that something was missing from their lives, which caused them unrest. When they found the lost piece, they could celebrate and have peace. But what if you feel they are lost forever? Or maybe they are just lost on earth for us to later find in heaven? I know I am looking forward to being reunited with my family and friends that have gone before me, as I am sure you are too. What a celebration that will be!

Some people are always searching for the missing piece in their lives they think will make them complete. What do you fill the missing pieces in with? I know a few of our finished puzzles have a missing piece or two. My husband and I have gotten creative on filling it with a fake piece and painting it as closely as possible to make it work, but I always know where it is. There's no replacement for that piece. How do you fill in that void to feel better or maybe not feel at all? Social media? TV? Drugs? Alcohol? I know when I feel down about something, I have to consciously decide not to avoid what I am feeling just because it's uncomfortable. It's easy to spiral downwards if you let yourself. These are the times you need to pick up a Bible or journal to help you refocus. "The human spirit was designed for relationship with God. If not divinely connected to Him in this way, we're left with a vacuum that can never be properly or completely filled. Like an intricately designed puzzle piece, the only true fit is the one true God."[28] This is where true peace is found.

Can some of your missing pieces always feel like they are missing? While I was trying to answer this question, I went for a walk at our Historic Arkansas Riverwalk of Pueblo to get some clarity. One of the quotes on a bench says, "Those we love don't go away, they walk beside us every day."[29] The pieces that are no longer with you for whatever reason have still shaped who you are today.

28 Priscilla Shirer, *Discerning the Voice of God*, p. 48.

29 Anonymous. Historic Arkansas Riverwalk of Pueblo bench, seen November 9, 2020.

A common saying is that people are in your life for a reason, a season, or a lifetime. You don't know when you meet them what category they will be given. Some seem like they are going to be around forever, but you lose touch over the years. Others that you may not click with right away become someone you confide in. That's one of the mysteries of life. It's okay to look back at the past to see how those people shaped you, but don't get stuck there. Be thankful for each missing piece in your puzzle because they make your puzzle more complete.

- *How have you chosen to remember your missing pieces?*

- *How have you found peace during a storm?*

- *How have your missing pieces made your puzzle more complete?*

WHAT'S YOUR FAITH SPEED?

"Note to self...The Bible says to keep my mind thinking on things above, not the things and troubles here on earth...to take control of my thoughts and point them to Christ. God's words will bring new life, hope and peace to my troubled situations. I must choose what I think about and focus on if I want to have peace."[30]

You can work on a puzzle at different speeds: 1. Fast when you are excited about it, 2. Slow when the pieces are slowly finding

---

30 @soyoureapastorswife, "Note to Self," Facebook, June 5, 2020, https://www.facebook.com/soyoureapastorswife/posts/2562044547392136.

their places, and 3. Stagnant when you feel you're stuck at a certain point. Your faith can also feel like it is operating at different speeds: when you feel you are on fire and willing to do whatever God wants you to do (unstoppable!), when you are just going through the motions, and when you are so shaken up that it can reset your focus completely. Or, like me, I felt like I experienced them all in the same year and sometimes even simultaneously.

Twenty-twenty was a crazy year for believers as we had to shift our focus from being in a church building to worshipping together however we could due to a pandemic. For me, though, I was still in the building because I was helping get the service out to our congregation. As the weeks and months went by, it became more about just going through the motions than enjoying the moment. I was constantly distracted by the camera angle, how it sounded, and if people were commenting about the service. We only missed a couple of Sundays, but I worried if everything was going well while we were away. In the same year, I also was on fire about this writing project. I would think about it a lot and was excited when I had time to work on it. It gave me such joy when something would come together smoothly that only God could have guided me. It was when I was writing that I felt the most connected with God. I enjoyed that time, even when I needed to fix parts of it or start a chapter from scratch.

So, what was the issue? I wasn't taking much time to just read the Bible, do a Bible study, or pray, which are ways to "fill our cup" and build our relationship with God. Instead, I was becoming rote in how I approached my faith: "mechanical or unthinking routine or repetition."[31] I was also becoming more and more

---

31 *Merriam-Webster's Dictionary*, https://www.merriam-webster.com/dictionary/rote, accessed Sept 15, 2021.

inflexible with anything that shook up my routine. I wanted everything to be perfect so that I could keep a mask on (pretend) that everything was fine with me. But, like all masks, we have to take them off at some point because God sees through them. I could keep my mask on with other people, but there's no faking it with God.

As people started coming back to church, I started to sink into the third speed and became stagnant. I only did what I was supposed to do: go to work and church and completed only the minimal chores at home. I had no energy or interest to do anything else, including writing. I had anxious thoughts (worries) and was angry at the smallest things. I knew I needed a few Sundays off, so I asked for a break from Worship Chair. My pastor agreed to give me eight weeks off. I felt a little better, but the struggle continued. As I tried to pry my hands open to let go of worrying about worship, the more I tried to hang on. It had been, even with the stress, a part of my routine that helped me through the pandemic. I journaled about some of my long-time fears and insecurities, like being rejected, being judged (for not doing things right), and not being in control.

Then, like when you get stuck on a puzzle, I felt like I didn't know what to do next. One Sunday, I went to church for the first time in a few weeks as just a participant. Feeling anxious and out of place the whole time, I took a walk after service and then tried journaling about why I was stuck. Ever tried to write when you feel stuck? Yeah, not much was happening. It can be like that when you pray as well. So, as I sat there, staring at the computer screen, I had a thought: "Rebuke Satan!" (This means to resist the devil/evil spirits' power to negatively influence me.) I don't know if I said it aloud or not, but right after that, I felt a huge weight lift off me and a rush of peace and joy flooded in. It took me aback, as I didn't fully understand what really happened. It then became clearer when I researched how evil spirits can influence someone. For me, it included broken confidence, distractions, stopping me from sharing my faith, taking joy out of my life, feeling apart from God and church members, feeling shame, guilt, rejection, doubt, fear, insecurity, and like a failure. He was also "inciting [me] to chase perfectionism instead of chasing God."[32] These were all things that evil spirits can plant. I was naïve to think it couldn't happen to me.

In the few days afterward, I felt like I had been given a second chance, like I had gone through another baptism and recommitted to my faith. It was a form of joy and peace that I hadn't ever felt, maybe because I had just been in a stronghold of negative emotions and was released in a moment. Unfortunately, a few days later, I was drawn back into a battle of trying to hold onto control when I was supposed to be on break. It is so easy to revert to what you have known because it's more comfortable than trusting God. I had just had a huge moment of joy, but like Peter when he denied Christ because he was afraid, I let fear try to take over again. I learned about a hedge of protection prayer based on Psalm 91, which I have prayed multiple times since. It makes me feel peace again and settles my mind.

The day of my rebuke, I remembered a Bible study I had done a few years ago, *The Armor of God* by Priscilla Shirer. The armor is the pieces to defend yourself from evil spirits. "Therefore put on the full armor of God, so that when the day of evil comes, you may be able to stand your ground, and after you have done everything,

---

32 Priscilla Shirer, *Armor of God*, (Nashville, Tennessee, LifeWay Press, 2015), p. 74.

to stand. Stand firm then, with the belt of truth buckled around your waist, with the breastplate of righteousness in place, and with your feet fitted with the readiness that comes from the gospel of peace. In addition to all this, take up the shield of faith, with which you can extinguish all the flaming arrows of the evil one. Take the helmet of salvation and the sword of the Spirit, which is the word of God" (Eph. 6:13-17). In this book, I keep referring to faith and peace, and while important, they are not the only things we need. We need to use all the pieces of the armor. They can help get you out of being stuck in stagnant speed. (If you are not familiar with the armor of God, I would highly recommend the Bible study I did to help you understand the pieces.)

Another lesson I learned during this time was to ask others to pray for me. Even after my moment of rebuke, I was still struggling. I asked my pastor to get some people to pray over me, which we did a few days later. I also received a prayer shawl, one that a church member had made and prayed over. I felt the comfort of knowing that there were people actively praying for me. I put the shawl on my bed, and those first few nights, I finally got some much-needed rest, both physically and mentally. It gave me more strength to get through and feel less ashamed to share with others that I was struggling. It also gave me peace because I didn't have to hide my true self (or keep the mask on). People would be there to help, support, and love me.

When we go through times of testing, we may wonder why. When I restarted the above study, I found a better way to describe my time of testing—sanctification. Priscilla describes it as "a process by which you are molded into the image of Christ. It's the

Spirit's progressive influence on you."[33] It's a process of putting aside things that are not pleasing to God and truly receiving the Word and peace of God. This time has made me more aware of what I should be doing and not doing to be a better example of Christ to others and actually trying better to live that out. Or as Priscilla describes later in the study, "Plain and simple, faith is an action."[34]

One of my favorite verses that I should have been using during this time is: "Do not be anxious about anything, but in every situation, by prayer and petition, with thanksgiving, present your requests to God. And the peace of God, which transcends all understanding, will guard your hearts and your minds in Christ Jesus" (Phil 4:6-7). It is easy to say don't be anxious about anything, but putting it into our daily routine can be a challenge. I have also heard to pray continually, which sounds overwhelming, but I found this quote that better describes it for me: "Prayer is a request for what is good, offered by the devout of God. But we do not restrict this request simply to what is stated in words…We should not express our prayer merely in syllables, but the power of prayer should be expressed in the moral attitude of our soul and in the virtuous actions that extend throughout our life…This is how you pray continually—not by offering prayer in words, but by joining yourself to God through your whole way of life, so that your life becomes one continuous and uninterrupted prayer."[35]

Even when I felt like I wasn't seeking God or that I didn't feel

---

33 Ibid, p. 88.

34 Ibid, p. 126.

35 St. Basil the Great, The Catalogue of Good Deeds, December 23, 2015, https://blog.obitel-minsk.com/2015/12/41-quotes-phrases-and-teachings-of.html, accessed June 17, 2021.

that strong of a connection, I kept serving God. He was always right there with me, showing me the way to peace. I am thankful I was able to learn how to be more aware of the next battle and be better prepared to fight it. It takes time to master taking every thought captive to Christ, so don't be discouraged if you don't do it quickly every time. Thankfully, with God on our side, we can overcome any fear and insecurity.

In these examples, the common theme was prayer. "Peace with God establishes our relationship with Him, and as a result, we can experience the peace of God."[36] It is through prayer that we build our relationship with God, turn from evil, and get the help we need to endure whatever situation that arises. There are going to be times when we all need a kickstart or a push to get our speed back up to unstoppable. If you seek peace with God and others, prayer is a great place to start!

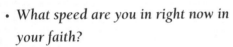

- *What speed are you in right now in your faith?*
- *Have you experienced both the peace with God and peace of God?*
- *What is your favorite Scripture about peace, and how can you use it to resist evil?*

---

36 Priscilla Shirer, *Armor of God*, p. 109.

TEN

COMPETITION VERSUS ENCOURAGEMENT

"Health does not always come from medicine.
Most of the time it comes from peace of mind,
peace in the heart, peace in the soul.
It comes from laughter and love."[37]

If you decide to do the puzzle with other people, are you excited or frustrated or even mad when another person places a piece? Do you try to one-up the other person to get ahead, even if you're working towards the same goal? You can do this in your

---

37 Operation Joy, @youinspirejoy, "Health Does Not Always Come From Medicine," Facebook, August 7, 2020,

life, starting when you are young, comparing your talents with siblings and peers, and later in life with job titles, how big your house is, and the list goes on. Do you acknowledge some people just have a natural talent for something and appreciate them for it, or does your competitive nature kick in? How can you put encouragement above your competitive spirit?

I would consider myself a competitive person when it comes to sports. In third grade, I started playing basketball and continued to play through high school. I am the youngest of three girls, and it was common for people to make comparisons between us. My middle sister also played basketball for several years, and it would drive me crazy when people would compare me to her. Sibling rivalry, for sure. Looking back, I can see that my competitiveness drove me to try harder. Competition can be good *only* if it doesn't cause harm to you or someone else.

My competitiveness almost caused me more harm than good while playing a sport I loved. In high school, I was the freshman team captain and had a great year. In my second year, I was on the junior varsity (JV) team and did well. I assumed, by the way things were going, that I would be on varsity for my junior year. To my disappointment, I was back on JV. I was sure they had made a mistake! However, after a few days of sulking, I decided to make the best of the situation and keep my commitment to the team.

Things were going fairly well until I rolled my ankle on a teammate's foot while getting a rebound. I knew it was bad. I hobbled off the court immediately and went to the trainer's room. My ankle had swelled up in just those couple of minutes. He checked it out and taped it up. I tried running on it. Nope. Not happening. I sat and iced my ankle while the game continued. I went to the doctor the next day and was told it was a bad sprain. It was what

I was dreading—my season was over. Or so I thought. I told my team the bad news, but I also decided to keep attending practices and games to support my teammates. As my ankle got stronger, I would do a little more and a little more. I then decided I would try to play in the last few games. My competitive spirit came out, but so did my faith. It would hurt in certain moments, but I helped it get stronger by continuing to try. I wasn't competing to be better than my sister anymore. It was to do the best that I could. I ended up playing in the last couple of games, and it was great to just get out there again. Even though I had already decided not to play the next year, even if my ankle was better, I wanted to finish the season I started. As I said, my faith was also being tested during the injury. I could have just said that it was too hard, and I wasn't going to try. I had to keep exercising my ankle to make it strong. Like working with my ankle, your faith can grow stronger the more you stretch yourself, even if it hurts or if it's only a little at a time. Every step you take draws you closer to peace in God.

Sometimes it's tempting to feel competitive if you compare your faith with other people's. Or think, I don't want to share because there are other people more knowledgeable or experienced or appear to have more faith than me, but God called all of us to share. This reminds me of a well-known saying: "God doesn't call the equipped, he equips the called." One way you equip yourself is by studying the Bible. Growing up, I don't remember doing Bible studies. While looking for a new church, I joined a Lenten Bible study. I felt like I could share my thoughts with my group, but we had one person who dominated the conversation. This discouraged me from wanting to try a new group.

However, several years ago, a women's Bible study class was offered, so I decided to give it another try. I am so glad because we have a great group of ladies that are welcoming and open to sharing. If I had let my first adult Bible study experience stop me from trying, I would have missed out on all the learning and bonding with others. I have learned so much about the Bible and myself through these studies. Even though I have attended many Bible studies, I still struggle to speak up and give my opinion. The important thing is that I haven't stopped going. I put the desire to keep learning above any discomfort I may feel. This gives me the peace to be okay with where I am in my faith. We can all strive to be better Christians, but it means looking at Christ and not at others.

Instead of competing, I would rather work with others on a team. In basketball, you have to rely on your teammates to be successful. You can't do it alone, even if you want to. You also have to be willing to help one another out if needed. In one game my freshman year, I had just stolen the ball from my opponent and was driving down the court to do a layup when my opponent pushed me. As I was on the ground, she stood over me, trying to get me to fight. I chose to get up and walk away, but one of my teammates was ready to jump in to defend me. Now, this girl was one of the sweetest people I had ever met, and she was willing to step in and help me. I will never forget how this felt. Looking back, I wasn't aware that I chose peace in that moment. I didn't let someone else determine whether I had peace or not.

You can take the team approach when looking at areas outside of sports, like a job or a committee at church or even putting a puzzle together. Unfortunately, you don't always get to choose who will be on your team. We all have people on our teams that appear to be ball hogs (or like to be the center of attention) or those who show up at a presentation without attending the prior meetings and try to take credit for all the work. Then there are those who you help who don't reciprocate. It can be frustrating in any of these situations to feel like you're working against a team member. The important thing to remember is to focus on the goal. Even if you may not have chosen who is on your team, you can learn from every person you meet.

Jesus knew who he wanted on his team, his disciples, even with all their flaws and frustrations. Even Jesus' disciples were competitive with each other when they were debating about who was the greatest. One of these debates happens at the Last Supper (see Luke 22). Can you imagine what Jesus was thinking? He had just told them he would be giving his life to save all people from sin and that one of them would betray him. All the disciples could think about was who would be the best. Jesus told them who would be the greatest: those who serve and are humble. I'm sure that's not what they wanted to hear. It can be difficult to understand why all the plays were called until the game is over, or like in the disciples' situation, it wasn't until Jesus died and was resurrected that all the pieces started to make sense. We can all learn from our mistakes, but hopefully, the coach doesn't have us running the same drills over and over until we learn the lesson.

Instead of being competitive, you can give encouragement to others. It takes no special talent to give a compliment. Things feel more manageable when we have the support of others. When one of my coworkers found out she was pregnant with her second child, my husband told me to suggest the name Barnabas as a possible choice. He grew up watching *Dark Shadows*, and the lead character was named Barnabas. So every time we talked about her pregnancy, I kept pushing for Barnabas. She hoped it was a girl so was disappointed when her ultrasound revealed she was having a boy. When she sent me the text message, I responded that Barnabas still had a chance. This made her laugh and feel a little less disappointed. The name Barnabas means son of encouragement, and in that moment, he did his job. I also gave her some information about St. Barnabas, seeing if I could influence her by pointing out he was a religious figure. After Saul, later known as Paul, saw Jesus on his way to Damascus and was called to preach the Good News, he went to Jerusalem to join the disciples. The disciples were afraid because Saul had been a persecutor of the Jews. Enter Barnabas. "But Barnabas took him and brought him to the apostles. He told them how Saul on his journey had seen the Lord and that the Lord had spoken to him, and how in Damascus he had preached fearlessly in the name of Jesus" (Acts 9:27). Barnabas' encouragement helped Saul on his first missionary trips. They were some of the first leaders of the church.

Fast forward to when her son was born (the name Barnabas was a no-go). I then told my mom the story. A few months later, she gave us a small stuffed dog named Barnabas on Christmas morning. I had to bring him to work a few days later to show everyone I now had my own Barnabas. Before he came to live with us, my mom shared the story with several friends. In response, I felt I needed to take pictures so they could see what he was up to. After I had taken several pictures, including at work, in the snow, and camping, I set up an Instagram page for him to share his exploits. It's a fun way to make people smile, even just for a minute. This world has enough stress and negativity that if I can give someone a little bit of light and hope, then I feel it's worth it. Barnabas has made a lot of new friends the past few years, and he's a good icebreaker with kids. He came along to my family get-togethers, and there have been several church members who wanted to see him at various things. As I said, if it makes people smile and forget their troubles for just a moment, it's worth the silliness of it all.

So, if you're given a choice to be a Barnabas and encourage someone else or your competitive spirit, please choose to be a Barnabas.

- *What brings out your competitive spirit? Are there times when it is a detriment to your faith?*

- *How can you be an encourager to someone else in your life, even a stranger?*

- *How can you be a better team player?*

ELEVEN

WILL YOU HELP ME?

"Refusing to release often means refusing to have peace."[38]

One thing you might do when working on a puzzle or project is to ask others for help. You may be used to helping others, which is good, but does that include helping yourself? Getting others to help you can give you a much-needed break. The benefits of these breaks include reconnecting with God, recharging, and refreshing your soul. Breaks can last from a few hours to several days. God is always with you to help you, but sometimes you need these breaks to strengthen your relationship with both God and other people.

---

38 Lysa Terkeurst, @proverbs31ministries, "Refusing to Release," Instagram, April 4, 2019, https://www.instagram.com/p/BvlWuZ8gyrS/?utm_source=ig_web_copy_link.

When I was doing scheduling, I didn't realize how often I checked both my work and personal phones until I gave up the work phone. Even when I wasn't on call, I still checked to make sure everything was running smoothly and responded to any messages to help the team. I was helping others, but I wasn't allowing myself the time to rest. In effect, I wasn't helping myself and had to walk away from that job. Time after time in the Bible, after the parable finishes, it says that Jesus went away—to a boat, to go pray, to move on to the next town. "Yet the news about him spread all the more, so that crowds of people came to hear him and to be healed of their sicknesses. But Jesus often withdrew to lonely places and prayed" (Luke 5:15-16). Jesus knew when he needed to take the time to reconnect with God and recharge. We can all learn from Jesus how not to push ourselves 24/7. You can find peace in those breaks.

One of my favorite places to go for a break and reconnect with God is the Great Sand Dunes National Park and Preserve near Alamosa, Colorado. On my first trip there, my husband and I decided we were going to try and hike to the highest peak. If you have ever hiked in sand, then you know how much harder it is than walking on a dirt or gravel trail. When we were ascending, it felt like two steps forward, sink in the sand, and one step back. Wow, what a workout. We made it a good way up, and I rested while Jeffrey proceeded to make it to the top. While I waited for him, I sat and took it all in. It was breathtaking. There was sand, water, snow-capped mountains, wind, clouds. A 360-degree view of beauty. I can't explain why it makes me feel so at peace while I'm there—it's just one of those places for me.

The place is unique because even if you return, you wouldn't be able to retrace your steps exactly, as the wind is constantly moving the sand and reshaping the dunes. The Holy Spirit is often described as wind. The Holy Spirit is always with you to help and guide you in experiences that will shape you. Most importantly, he is there when you feel like you're climbing a mountain of sand (or going through a difficult time) by yourself. Sometimes it can feel like a light breeze (little nudge). Other times, it can be more like a big gust, which can include a life-changing decision. Hopefully, we can all use the Holy Spirit's guidance in our lives. Like the sand dunes, when you look back at who you were, you can see how you have changed. Other people may not be able to see what footsteps you may have taken in the past, but they will see where the steps have led you. Each step is important to reach the peak of who you were meant to be, which leads to peace. It's important to take those moments to reflect, reconnect, and refresh.

While at the Sand Dunes, I couldn't help but think of Moses leading the people in the desert. What were their conditions like for those forty years? In the book of Numbers, Moses had ordered spies to check out the land of Canaan, the land promised to the Israelites, and their report back was full of fear. In reality, it was more of a lack of trust in God. This was after they had crossed the Red Sea on dry land and God provided water, manna, and quail to sustain them. Yet, there was still fear. They didn't trust that God would help them when they entered the land he had promised them. "For forty years—one year for each of the forty days you explored the land—you will suffer for your sins and know what it is like to have me against you" (Num. 14:34). Those forty years must have been difficult, but also reassuring. God took care of the people that were still alive. God could have given up on them, but his love for his people was greater.

In 2020, I turned forty, which made me think about how many days that amounted to for the Israelites in the desert—my whole life so far. When you look at it that way, it puts life's challenges in perspective. There have been difficult moments, but God has been there with me and taken care of me. When I googled how many times the number forty was in the Bible, I was surprised to see how many instances there were: ones I knew like Noah and the flood and Jesus' temptation, both lasting forty days. There were also ones I didn't know, like the three main kings of Israel—Saul, David, and Solomon—all ruled for forty years. What they all had in common was "Scripturally speaking—'forty means something', as it brings to mind such qualities as *repentance, newness, preparation* (say for an important work or task), *self-examination, transformation, task fulfillment, escape from bondage or slavery* (such as to sin), *nourishment and growth* (for example, in the spiritual life), and, finally, *personal fulfillment*, such as with *redemption* and *salvation*, and ultimately, *new generation* and *new life*."[39] So, in short, I really should not have been surprised that this writing project really took off only a month after I turned forty. All those qualities mentioned above have helped prepare me for this new adventure of doing God's will.

Most people feel God's presence and peace when out in nature, such as on a hike or watching the waves crash onto the beach, but the real challenge is to find those moments in everyday life. A short break where we can reflect on the goodness of God's provision in our lives can refresh us, such as looking through old photos and letters. For me, this also includes my old writing. I am so glad I have kept these entries so I can look back and discover

---

39 Father Wade Menezes, "Significance of '40' in Sacred Scripture," March 4, 2021, https://fathersofmercy.com/the-significance-of-40-in-scripture/, accessed May 9, 2021.

new things I had not seen before. Back in 1999, I took a summer poetry class to improve my writing skills. The last page of my class journal was a reflection on what I learned during the class. I ended the page with: "I'm young and I've got time to develop myself as a writer, as long as I keep patience and confidence in myself. I know there will be hard times, but I know I've made a good decision to write because that release through writing is something that nothing else can do." My teacher then wrote, in part, "You are on your path…and you are a true writer." What a way to refresh my soul! What's amazing to me is while I had been looking for my voice while writing this book, I had already found it. God has helped me by putting people in my life to encourage me on my entire path. I hope that you also have those encouragers that are and/or were in your life.

One way you can help and encourage others and connect with God is to go on a mission trip. The goal is to spread the gospel and show God's love to others, which often includes helping others. I have gone on two mission trips—one to Yakima, Washington, with my youth group and one to Greensburg, Kansas, with my current church. What wonderful experiences helping a family, bonding with others in Christ, and yes, hard work. Even though we were tired at the end of the week, it was also energizing.

My small group in Yakima had to paint the entire interior of a house, which was a challenge. I think we managed to finish it, with help from a paint gun towards the end. The most energizing part was the last night when we were invited to go to a Pow-Wow. Since we had been working on the reservation, I was intrigued to check it out. The people's garments and dances were amazing, but the most touching piece was when our group was asked if we wanted to join in on a dance. It was a simple side-step dance with two circles that went in opposite directions, and you shook hands as you went. The announcer saw us and found out we were from the workcamp and told the crowd about what we had been doing. When he saw us come around, he said, "There go those Christians again." I think after the announcer said who we were, many more people joined the dance and shook our hands. I felt as if I was accepted into their culture, and their handshakes were the best way to say thank you. Wow. What a moment of human connectedness at its core. If you ever get a chance to go on a mission trip, take it. It's one of the best ways to take a break from our regular routines and the ruts we sink into. It is also a great way to strengthen our relationships with other people and God. You can then take the joy and peace from the experience back with you to your job, church activities, and even simple daily interactions with others.

Sometimes when you are overwhelmed with a task, it can feel easier to just give up. You can re-assess the pros and cons of each decision when you take a step back. If you find peace in the decision to continue that task, then you can recommit and move forward. There is also nothing wrong with asking others for help. It can be difficult and even humbling to ask someone else to help you, especially if you view asking for help as a sign of weakness. When you ask others for help, a burden is lifted because you no longer feel like you have to do it all on your own. Other people may think that you don't need or want help, so you may have to take the initiative to ask. You may even have to include people you haven't worked with before. It is refreshing to see other people get involved in a project or task. You can even build a relationship with someone you didn't expect. Don't forget to ask God for help, for he alone can provide peace and strength. It feels less overwhelming when you know you have help and peace from God in all tasks. This can give you the confidence and strength that will show through to others. Don't be afraid to ask!

- *Where is your favorite place to refresh and reconnect with God?*

- *Where can you find the peace of God in everyday life?*

- *How can you draw strength from God to ask others for help?*

TWELVE

PATIENTLY WAITING?

"Let nothing disturb you;
Let nothing frighten you.
All things are passing.
God never changes.
Patience gains all things.
Nothing is wanting to him who possesses God.
God alone suffices."[40]

There are times when you're working on a puzzle or any time-consuming project and think you'll never finish. Fortunately, the

---

40 Amy , *The Salt Stories*, "St. Theresa of Avila, Making New Friends in Heaven," October 15, 2015, http://thesaltstories.com/st-teresa-of-avila-making-new-friends-in-heaven/, accessed May 9, 2021.

further along you are, the easier it is to build momentum. But what happens when you are forced to wait for something to happen, like if you were only given half of the puzzle pieces? Would you look at the added puzzle pieces as a blessing or a new challenge? Sometimes, you want to speed up time until you get all the pieces in place. Isn't it true that in the waiting, you need the patience to persevere?

One goal that took patience and perseverance was getting out of debt. In 2009, my husband and I went through Dave Ramsey's Financial Peace University. We tracked our spending through a budget. It was tough to tell ourselves no, so we could pay off our debts and save for emergencies. In the class, step two of seven is when you list your debts, smallest to largest, and then focus on paying off the lowest amount first (while still paying the minimum on the rest). If we had been told to tackle all seven steps at once, it would have been overwhelming, like putting a thousand-piece puzzle together without ever having solved a puzzle before. But, as we paid off each debt, we gained momentum, which motivated us to continue.

When I decided to quit my job without something else lined up, we had our three-month emergency fund and were working on paying off our house. (For those who know the baby steps, we were on steps four [save for retirement] and six [pay off our house]). I felt assured that we would be okay because as Jesus said, "Therefore I tell you, do not worry about your life, what you will eat or drink; or about your body, what you will wear. Is not life more than food and the body more than clothes?" (Matt 6:25). Wait, what? Not worry? Most of us could be professional worriers. I put my trust in God that we would be okay and found peace in that trust.

We have since paid off our house, which has been a blessing (puzzle piece completed). However, I didn't know then that we would be faced with a new challenge: to avoid the temptation of going back into debt. In some ways, it is easier to rationalize not getting something you want because you don't have the resources. It had been a long time since either of us had been out of debt, and it was an adjustment. Even with adjustments, I would encourage you to get out of debt because truly, "No one can serve two masters. Either you will hate the one and love the other, or you will be devoted to the one and despise the other. You cannot serve both God and money" (Matt 6:24). There is a level of peace that comes with not having debt, but you still need a lot of patience to save for those items you want.

Another example of being forced to wait for something to happen is when our church was searching for a new pastor. In our denomination, we prepared a description of what our congregation was looking for, read through potential pastor applications (called profiles), interviewed candidates on the phone and in person, and then the congregation voted for the pastor. There was a search team that went through all these steps together. I was asked to be on our most recent team. The search process can take up to three years for a permanent pastor, which can feel like a long time. We started the process thinking we would focus on finding a permanent pastor and have guest preachers every week in the meantime. One of those guest preachers approached our search team leader to offer to be our interim pastor. What a blessing that was. It wasn't what we were expecting to happen, but it was a wonderful gift, like getting more pieces to our puzzle. This gave us more time to find the right person and not feel as rushed. It also gave us the energy and drive to persevere to complete our original challenge. There were many times when I felt impatient with this process and had to remind myself of the end goal. If our team had just chosen the first person we received an application from, yes, we could have been done, but would it have been successful? Most likely not.

Several months after our interim pastor started, our team thought we had selected the right candidate and were close to that finish line (puzzle piece almost placed). Unfortunately, the candidate backed out right before the congregational meeting. It was heartbreaking to get that close and fall short, but God had a better plan. That experience unified our church and strengthened the members' support for our team, which was so reassuring. We had the faith and trust of our church members to be successful, which were major factors in our perseverance to complete our task. In God's time, our team found the right fit for our church. Even though it felt like we were forced to wait, something better came out of it than we even expected. "Since God has planned something better for us so that only together with us would they be made perfect" (Heb. 11:40).

During the search process, I wrote a blog about waiting. I decided to wait until the next morning to reread it and then post it. The problem was that when I went to look for it, it wasn't saved. Ironically, the post about waiting shouldn't have been put off to be shared. Isn't that true about waiting? You can wait too long to live out a dream or tell someone how you feel, and then you regret not doing it. My original thought for the blog was we can wait until we think our lives will be the most exciting or fulfilling to do something. My hope is that if you feel compelled to live out a dream or life goal, you pray about it, and if you get the green light, don't wait. Start now!

However, sometimes your calling from God can include a time of waiting. You feel you have been called to do something, but then things get in your way, or you only get small clues. It is also possible that God, in his timing, may force you to wait. A Biblical example was when David was anointed to be the next king of Israel. He had to wait many years to actually see that calling fulfilled. Another way to look at it is best described by Priscilla Shirer when she says, "Waiting is not the same as inactivity. Waiting is a commitment to continue in obedience until God speaks."[41] David was obedient and was seen as "a man after his [God's] own heart" (1 Sam 13:14).

A song that comes to my mind that shows us what to do when we're waiting, hopefully patiently, is "While I'm Waiting." The lyrics talk about the pain of waiting, but also about pushing ahead to keep worshipping and being hopeful while you're waiting. One of the lines is, "I'm waiting on you Lord and I am peaceful."[42] This means you can find peace, even when you want something to happen right now.

There are many examples of people who patiently waited on God in the Bible. One of the lesser-known examples is the story of Shadrach, Meshach, and Abednego in the book of Daniel. King Nebuchadnezzar had built an idol of himself and wanted everyone to bow down to it. Shadrach, Meshach, and Abednego did not follow this decree, as they only worshipped God. The king was furious and sent them to the fiery furnace. They said, "If we are thrown into the blazing furnace, the God we serve is able to deliver us from it, and he will deliver us from Your Majesty's hand. But

---

41 Priscilla Shirer, *Discerning the Voice of God*, p. 149.
42 John Waller, "While I'm Waiting," Track 8 on *The Blessing*, Beach Street Records, 2009, Compact Disc.

even if he does not, we want you to know, Your Majesty, that we will not serve your gods or worship the image of gold you have set up" (Dan. 3:17-18). These three showed ultimate trust in God and were okay with either outcome. Whether they lived or died, they were willing to stand up for what they believed in. God saw their trust in him, and they were able to walk out of the furnace completely unhurt. This opened the eyes of the king to trust their God. They didn't waiver from their faith and waited on God to save them. "Consider it pure joy, my brothers and sisters, whenever you face trials of many kinds, because you know that the testing of your faith produces perseverance" (James 1:2-3). There will be times in your life that you will face trials, but you can and will get through them. "Sometimes God will keep you from the fire. Other times God will make you fireproof and take you through the fire."[43]

You may never know why you're asked to wait. We've become so accustomed to instant gratification, like my dogs getting their treats. We want it all right now!! But, if you look closely, there's always a reason, or at least a lesson, in waiting. You may learn that what you thought you wanted wasn't what you were supposed to have or be. So, whether you are forced to wait for something to happen or have to push yourself to complete a project, know that you are not alone in this life. You can lean on the support of others and from God to get to whatever that end goal might be. It may not be at the exact time that you had hoped it would be, and you probably have to wait, so here is something you can wait for:

"Wait for the Lord; be strong and take heart and wait for the Lord" (Ps. 27:14).

---

43 Apostolic Holiness, @apostolicholinessah, Facebook, March 3, 2021, https://www.facebook.com/ApostolicHolinessAH/posts/3604550609643431.

- What was something you had to wait for? How did you find peace in the waiting?

- When did you get something better because you had to wait?

- What event/time in your life did God bring you through the fire and make you fireproof (and at peace)?

THIRTEEN

FINISH STRONG

*"To walk by faith is to continue moving forward in the things
God has called you to and believing God for good always.
Walking by faith means that you trust the Lord so much, you
obey and you step out of your comfort zone to do what he asks,
even when you aren't sure what the outcome will be, knowing
God will protect you and provide for you! (2 Cor. 9:8)"*[44]

When you get that last piece in, what do you do with the finished puzzle? Do you sit and admire it for a while or even glue it

---

44 Christine Caine, @christinecaine, "To Walk By Faith is to Continue Moving forward,"
Facebook, January 28, 2019, https://www.facebook.com/permalink.php?story_fbid=
10161523908915089&id=143678730088.

together and frame it? When you finish, you can see which parts were challenging and know you made it through them. Do you rip it apart, vowing to never do another one? Do you pass it onto someone else? What do you do with other finished projects, like paintings or writings or quilts? You share them, right? So why should that be any different with your faith?

When I think of sitting and admiring an accomplishment, it reminds me of hiking up a mountain peak. Even though I live in Colorado, I haven't attempted a 14,000-foot mountain hike, a 14er, yet. However, there is a hike that I can say was an accomplishment. The Music Pass Trail to Upper Sand Creek Lake starts with hiking up to Music Pass, where you can enjoy the view for a moment, but it's not your final stop. To hike to one of the two lakes, you actually descend from that pass down and then back up to the chosen lake. However, whether you remember or not, you have to hike back up on your way back. And it feels much steeper, maybe because you are already tired from hiking the few miles to the lake and back to that point. It takes determination to get back to the top.

You will have mountain highs and valley lows throughout your life. Sometimes it's taking one day at a time, or even one hour at a time, to get through whatever difficulty you are tackling. Once you get through it, you can look back and see how far you have come, like a finished puzzle. As Tyler Perry wrote, "Even though you haven't reached your goal yet, with each step you are getting closer. Don't think about the finish line. Enjoy the race! Don't allow yourself to become overwhelmed with how far you still have to go. Focus on one step at a time. Be grateful for how far you've come. Thank God for where you are. Keep going."[45] What was the finish

---

45 Tyler Perry, *Higher is Waiting*, (New York, New York, Penguin Random House LLC, 2017), p. 62.

line on this hike? The first time we got to the peak, the lake, or back to the peak? The true accomplishment was the entire journey, ending with getting safely back home.

Nothing gives us the true sense of peace in accomplishing something than when we are doing God's will and fulfilling our calling. This includes saying yes to tasks you don't believe you can do on your own. One final way I walked out my faith, literally, was when my youth group had a task on Good Friday. We carried a large and heavy wooden cross around our town before bringing it in during the church service as a way to honor Jesus. There were several of us who took turns carrying the cross, a few at a time. Did I mention the cross was heavy? At one point, we realized we needed to move at a faster pace to make it to the church at the specified time. Our youth group leader, Brendan, took the cross, and somehow, I was the only other one helping him carry it. What I don't remember is complaining about how heavy it was or how much further we had to go or if it was painful. We had a goal in mind, and that was all we needed. You can look at the cross you have been given to bear. Your attitude towards that cross can make all the difference in the world. It also gives you peace if you have people and Jesus in your life that can be there for you if it becomes too much for you. Simon of Cyrene was called to help Jesus carry the cross. Even if we may not know what effect that had on Simon's life, it made all the difference for Jesus to fulfill God's will.

We can hope, when we look back at our life, to be like Paul, who said, "I have fought the good fight, I have finished the race, I have kept the faith" (2 Tim. 4:7). Since you are not at the finish line yet, I challenge you to take your own steps of faith and share your faith in whatever way you feel you can. One way I challenged my fellow church members a few years ago was to give them a token that said, "Peace I leave with you; my peace I give you" (John 14:27). It was my piece of peace challenge for them to give to someone else who they felt called to give it to. This is just one way you can start a conversation and be a peacemaker in this troubled world. The best news is that Jesus said, "'I have told you these things, so that in me you may have peace. In this world you will have trouble. But take heart! I have overcome the world'" (John 16:33).

When I started this writing project, I came across a movie called *Puzzle*, which was about puzzle competitions. One quote that stuck out to me was, "There's nothing we can do to control anything. But when you complete a puzzle, when you finish it, you know that you have made all the right choices. No matter how many wrong pieces you tried to fit into a wrong place, but at the very end, everything makes one perfect picture. What other pursuits can give you that kind of perfection? Faith? Ambition? Wealth? Love? No. Not even love can do that, Mata. Not completely."[46] What struck me was what I disagreed with: that love couldn't give us perfection. Jesus loved us so much that he gave his life so we could all be made perfect. "For by one sacrifice he has made perfect forever those who are being made holy" (Heb 10:14).

Why do we read Bible verses over and over? For the same reason, we watch the same movies over and over. We laugh or cry over the same scene, even though we know what happens, like the funeral scene in *My Girl*. Tears every time! We anticipate our favorite scenes like our favorite verses. We recite lines. Most movies have a happy ending, and so does the Bible. Jesus is coming soon! How can you top that? One day, our friends gave us tickets to a Casting Crowns concert. It was a great night of praising

---

46 *Puzzle*, directed by Marc Turtletaub, Big Beach Olive Productions, 2018.

God with many people. Their final song still sticks in my mind: "Glorious Day." The chorus of the song is:

Living, He loved me
Dying, He saved me
Buried, He carried my sins far away
Rising, He justified freely forever
One day He's coming
Oh glorious day, oh glorious day[47]

What a glorious day that will be! When Jesus was on the cross, his final words were, "It is finished" (John 19:30) and then he took his last breath. Even though you may finish a puzzle, a project, a book, or a job, you take these experiences with you. The finish line for all of us is to make it safely home to heaven. Until then, we are all called to keep sharing the love of Christ with others in our own unique ways.

The first step of faith is the hardest, but go ahead and take it. It may make all the difference "for such a time as this" (Esther 4:14).

There is only one question left to ask:

- *How can you share the love of Christ with others and finish strong?*

---

47 Casting Crowns, "Glorious Day (Living He Loved Me)," Track 6 on *Until the Whole World Hears*, Reunion Records, 2009.

ORIGINAL BLOG POST

When you put together a puzzle, you study the pieces, their shape, size, and color. You can look at the box with the finished picture to know in what section it may go. Sometimes the pieces don't seem like they fit, like they may have been put in the wrong box.

We are all pieces in the big puzzle called life. We have many pieces in our lives that may not seem to fit together, so we try piece after piece, even ones we know won't work, to see what fits. Sometimes it seems like we've tried the same piece over and over, but it's also about timing. God's timing is always perfect. We are here at this time of life for a reason and all the pieces are perfectly arranged. All the pieces come together to make something beautiful. We can't see the full picture, but God knows the end from the beginning.

We rely on the pieces that are closest to us to make the bigger picture complete. But we also rely on those pieces that don't seem to fit in our lives to make us who we are. We also can't get rid of the pieces we don't like because the picture will not be complete.

The puzzle is only done when all the pieces are interlocked to each other, touching at least two other pieces. We have to work together to make it complete by staying connected. If not, we'll all just be lonely single pieces again. We are all important pieces of the big puzzle of life!